YOUR GUIDE TO

BETTER

DELEGATING

DISCOVER THE SECRETS TO BECOMING
MORE EFFECTIVE TOMORROW
THAN YOU ARE TODAY.

Volume 2

OF

THE EFFECTIVENESS GUIDE

BY

EDWARD J. MURPHY

Never STOP Learning!

WHAT OTHERS SAY ABOUT
The Effectiveness Institute

"I highly recommend the books from The Effectiveness Institute as texts for new leaders and a review for seasoned leaders - as a reminder of what they should be doing. These books are unique because they're replete with valuable information that you can actually learn today and use tomorrow. If you want to become absolutely essential to any organization, these books are for you."

- Dennis D. Cavin
Lieutenant General, US Army (Retired)
Vice President Army and Missile Defense Programs
Lockheed Martin, Corporate Business Development

"I recommend the books from The Effectiveness Institute because Ed Murphy doesn't theorize; he draws on his extensive experience from many years of service in the US Military and from working as an Executive Coach in Corporate America. His keen insights and practical advice make these books required reading for anyone trying to negotiate the maze of organizational chaos."

- Lee Lacy
Assistant Professor
US Army Warfighter Book
Command and General Staff College

"The books from The Effectiveness Institute will help you become more effective at work and in life. They will also help you unlock your potential and direct your team to greater success. I highly recommend these books."

- Lance Revo
Principal Engineering Design Specialist
Cyber Security at AREVA NP

I DEDICATE

THIS BOOK

TO

My Favorite Nephew,

ROBERT J. CHASE

*"Rob, I won't be around during your lifetime. But
if I were, I'd tell you exactly what's in this book.
That's why I wrote it. May it bless you and your posterity
to find true joy and enhance the quality of your life.
Make a difference in the lives of others by adding value
to them in some meaningful way, and you'll be
richly rewarded in this life and in the next.
Know that I'm always with you!
Much love always."*

Other Books From
THE EFFECTIVENESS INSTITUTE

Here are the eleven volumes from *The Effectiveness Institute*, one for each Core Competencies of Effectiveness:

VOLUME 1: The Power of FOLLOWERSHIP

VOLUME 2: The Power of DELEGATING

VOLUME 3: The Power of PLANNING

VOLUME 4: The Power of ORGANIZING

VOLUME 5: The Power of COMMUNICATING

VOLUME 6: The Power of PROBLEM-SOLVING

VOLUME 7: The Power of AWARENESS

VOLUME 8: The Power of TRAINING

VOLUME 9: The Power of MOTIVATION

VOLUME 10: The Power of CHARACTER

All the above books are available at *Amazon.com*

Never STOP Learning!

This page is intentionally left blank.

CONTENTS

PREFACE

I'm often asked, "What does the picture mean on the cover of your book?"

This picture is a metaphor for the dilemma young people face when coming from school to the world-of-work.

They're unprepared, do not have the right tools, the right motivation, nor any clue of what's most important to every employer on the planet.

The cover image shows a young man rowing a boat in the fog. If you look closer, you'll notice that the boat is too small for the person in it. You can tell because one side of the boat is dipping so low in the water that it's almost taking on water. You can also tell that he has little experience in a boat because the other side is way out of the water because his weight is not evenly distributed.

He is also rowing in dense fog. He cannot see where he's going. The further he gets from shore; he cannot turn around and head back because he has no idea from which direction he came.

Finally, since he's not wearing a flotation device, he's assuming he won't have to swim. You know where assumptions take you, right? He is totally unprepared.

He didn't plan his trip, nor is he prepared to deal with the consequences of what lies ahead. He is, or will soon be, lost and at the mercy of nature.

Such is the fate of young workers today.

In today's job market, there's a huge skills gap between graduation and the first day on the job. As a result, young people lack the job skills needed to *"hit-the-ground-running"* and find themselves in dead-end, menial, minimum-wage jobs, trading time for money just to put food on the table. And it will take them decades before they're effective enough to *add value* to any employer. What a waste!

How do I know that? I know it because I've spent 20+ years of my life as an executive coach, working with hundreds of business executives and small business owners, seeking the answer to this simple question:

Why are some people more effective than others?

What do they think, say, and do that make them more effective?

During that time, I was privileged to work with some of America's most exceptional men and women. Through their example, I learned the true definition of effectiveness by documenting what they did, how they did it, and most importantly, how they made people feel. What you'll find here is the result of my years of research.

Today, my purpose in life is to help you navigate the *world-of-work*, maximize your true career potential, and become more effective and successful at work and in life.

PS: Can you tell which way he's rowing? Is he rowing towards or away from the camera? Hint: Look closely at the hand closest to the water.

ENJOY!

INTRODUCTION

"Surround yourself with the best people you can find, delegate authority, and don't interfere as long as the policy you've decided upon is being carried out."
- Ronald Reagan

This book is about **DELEGATING!**

Delegating is your ability to enable others to act on your behalf to get more done faster than you ever could on your own.

Delegating is also one of these eleven Core Competencies of your effectiveness and success at work and in life.

Followership, Delegating, Planning, Organizing, Communicating, Problem-Solving, Decision-Making, Awareness, Training, Motivating and Character.

This book is for everyone in the workforce who reports to another person for their work assignments, including employees working for an employer and small business owners, entrepreneurs, and the self-employed working for customers, clients, or patients.

Simply stated, this book is for you regardless of your occupation, position, or level of authority.

You may not realize that *Delegating* is one of the most important components of your effectiveness and success at work. If you fail to delegate many of your duties and responsibilities to a Direct Report, you'll never have the time to devote to your more pressing boss only *Inherent Expectations* (Chapter 7), and you'll lose your *Flexibility to Respond* (Chapter 11), which will lead to your demise. *Rookie Mistake!*

This happens because you know you can do these things quicker and easier than anyone else, and you fear that someone else will *drop-the-ball.*

Many Delegators don't understand the damage they're doing by not trusting their members and training them to make things happen on their behalf.

They're also clueless to uncovering hidden expectations, managing risk by conducting a risk assessment, anticipating unintended consequences, 2d and 3d order effects, eliminating unresolved issues, or collaborating to build consensus with a team - all of which are addressed in this book.

Without these abilities, you'll be wasting your career sitting on the sidelines, watching others move ahead while wondering why?

I speak from 24 years as a US Army Officer and 20 years as an Executive Coach in Corporate America in Seattle, San Diego, Kansas City, and Phoenix.

As an Executive Coach, I was blessed to work with some of America's most successful men and women, including hundreds of business executives, teams, and small business owners.

I documented what they said, did, how they did it, what worked and what didn't. But, most importantly, I documented how they made people feel.

As a result, I learned that the most effective and successful people stood out because they were able to do these two things better than anyone else:

- First, to consistently produce excellent results.
- Second, to add value to those who helped produce those results.

This book will enhance your ability to do both.

The fact is that you may be the top producer, but if you haven't added value to those who helped you, especially your boss, you'll never become effective or successful, period.

What new skills or abilities have you acquired in the last twelve months? What contributions have you made to your current position since this time last year?

And, most of all, what are you doing about it?

This book is unique because it:

- Gives you the most actionable tactics, techniques, and tools needed to consistently produce excellent results.
- Teaches you the best practices used every day by the most effective and successful people in their field, which you were never taught in school.
- Provides you with step-by-step instructions explaining what and how things should be done that you won't find anywhere in

academia or Corporate America to help you maximize your true potential.

- Contains everything you want to know about *Delegating*, plus everything you didn't realize you need to know about how *Delegation* enhances your effectiveness and success in business.

I know that by learning, using, and sharing the best practices found here, you'll be well on your way to becoming more effective and successful.

Remember, no matter how good you think

you are; you can always be better.

So, what are you waiting for? You have too much to lose by not taking a more active role in your Professional Development.

When you're ready to *elevate-your-game* to the next level, join us on this incredible *Journey of Discovery.*

Also, if you feel this information could help someone else, please let them know. If it turns out to make a difference in their life, they'll be forever grateful to you, as will I.

Never STOP Learning!

Ed

Founder of *The Effectiveness Institute*

email: ed.murphy77@gmail.com

Stop wishing you were better and do something about it today!

This page is intentionally left blank.

1
THE POWER OF
DELEGATING

"I want someone where I have confidence and credibility that they're up to the job and that I can trust what they tell me."
- Karl Rove

This book will give you a far better understanding of *Delegation*, its definition, importance, and how to do it successfully.

Delegating is your ability to enable others to act on your behalf to get more done faster than you ever could on your own.

Here, you'll learn to use the most actionable *tactics, techniques, and tools* needed to master the *Art of Delegating*.

As an executive coach for over 20 years, I know what your boss and customers expect, especially when it comes to your effectiveness and success at work.

Effective people know that their ability to delegate is critical to their effectiveness and success at work. By learning, using, and sharing these *best practices*, you'll be well on your way to becoming the one person who adds the greatest value to the team - making you essential.

Also, to make thisbook easier to understand, I'll use the term "boss" instead of leader, employer, or customer. I do this because if you're an employee, your boss is your employer. And if you're self-employed or a small business owner, your boss is your customer, client, or patient.

This means that you'll always be working for a boss - whoever pays you for your products or services.

This also means that you'll always be a follower of someone - whoever pays you for your work.

So, let's get to work!

Delegation empowers a follower to make decisions. It drives decision-making authority from one level to a lower one. However, if done right, the delegation isn't abdication because the delegator is still responsible and accountable for the outcome of the assignment.

The delegator can never assign or transfer their responsibility or accountable for their assignment.

In the business world, delegation grants or transfers authority from a delegator to a follower to accomplish an assignment. However, the delegator is still responsible and accountable for the follower's acts or omissions in carrying out the purpose of the assignment.

Effective people also know that they can never consistently produce excellent results without developing, nurturing, and enabling team members to act on their behalf. This empowers a follower to act independently with proper resources to accomplish an assignment.

The delegator doesn't have to be a boss or someone with authority.

Delegators are often peers, friends, or even spouses. Delegation saves money, time, motivates team members, and creates more effective teams.

Delegating an assignment isn't abdication because the asker is still responsible and accountable for the end-result.

5% of delegating is asking someone to perform a task by a certain time. The other 95% is about following up to ensure it gets done.

2
BY BUILDING
TRUST

"Few things can help an individual more than to place responsibility on him, and to let him know that you trust him."
- Booker T. Washington

Trust is the glue that holds everything together for any company. Trust is important in business because it forms the basis of all relationships and interactions.

Trust is the firm belief in the reliability, honesty, integrity, ability, or strength of someone.

Creating a sense of trust is the most important factor when considering team member performance. Successful businesses are built on relationships, and the foundation of all relationships is trust. Unfortunately, there may be times when some people may not see eye to eye.

However, if members treat each other with respect and kindness and can get their ideas across without feeling belittled or discriminated against, then trust can be built. Without trust, the ability to agree or build consensus will always be compromised.

What are the benefits of trust?

- Increases productivity and improves morale.
- Enables members to work more effectively as a team.
- Reduces the time to discuss key issues and make decisions.
- Facilitates cooperation and collaborative problem-solving.
- Produces improved effectiveness and diminishes costs.
- Expands allegiance and sustainability.

Trust is the emotional component of companionship, friendship, love, agreement, relaxation, and comfort.

Why are some bosses reluctant to delegate?

The main phobia bosses have about delegating is losing control. I get it. However, the truth is that you never had control in the first place.

Control over other people is an illusion!

But, influence, through persuasion, is achievable.

The sooner you realize this fact, the quicker you'll achieve order from chaos and let others do their job. The key to delegating is to do so gradually until you know who can move the work forward and who can't.

Are there different degrees of trust?

This list show is the different degrees of trust, starting with showing *very little trust* and ending with showing *complete trust*:

- Bring the facts to me for action (little trust).

- Develop alternatives, and I'll take action based on the facts.

- Be prepared to take action, but don't do anything until I say so.

- Tell me what you propose to do and when.

- Analyze the situation, take action, and tell me the results.

- Just go! Here's the situation, deal with it! (complete trust).

How do you build trust?

Do you know the most important components of building relationships? You shouldn't be surprised that it's trust. How much does your boss trust you? How much trust do you have in your team members?

Here are the important components of building trust:

- If others sense that you're AUTHENTIC, you're much more likely to be trusted.

- If others sense that your LOGIC is solid, you're far more likely to be trusted.

- If others sense your EMPATHY is sincere and directed at them, you're far more likely to be trusted.

When all three are present, you have their trust. But if any one of these three is missing or needs work, trust is in question.

How can you become more Authentic?

In human relations, your lack of authenticity is considered bad faith in dealing with other people.

Authenticity is the degree to which your actions are congruent with your beliefs and desires, despite external pressures to conform.

You'll tend to hold back who you are for fear that someone might dislike you. You may even go so far as to be more like those with whom you work, hoping to fit in. Unfortunately, all this only makes you less likely to be trusted. Pay less attention to what other people think about you and more attention to what you think about yourself.

We all have an obligation to set and maintain the conditions that not only make it safe to be authentic but make it welcome. It's the key to achieving greater effectiveness. How do you do it? You do it by being yourself and treating everyone with respect and kindness.

How can you use Logic?

Logic is the study of correct reasoning, especially as it involves the drawing of inferences.

Logic has two gates that you must pass through to be acceptable.

- It must be rational, reasonable, and doable.

- It must be communicated in a manner that's easily understood, straightforward, and supported with evidence.

How can you show Empathy?

Empathy is the capacity to understand or feel what another person is experiencing and the capacity to place oneself in another's position.

There are two levels of empathy: Cognitive and Affective.

- **Cognitive empathy** means that you're capable of understanding other people's thoughts and feelings.

- **Affective empathy,** in addition to understanding, means that you're capable of feeling other people's emotions and of sharing their grief, suffering, and joy.

In addition to creating trust, these three skills can help you build an emotional connection with others and truly relate to their feelings. Empathy can be learned to help bring you closer to having greater success in your relationships.

3
BY KNOWING WHAT
BOSSES NEED TO SURVIVE

"It takes half your life before you discover
life is a do-it-yourself project."
- Napoleon Hill

Every effective boss needs effective followers who can resolve problems and achieve goals. And any effective follower knows how to turn any assignment (a problem, goal, event, or activity) into a simple project and manage that project to completion.

As far as your boss is concerned, your effectiveness or value-added is a function of your ability to manage projects. And you don't need to be a *certified project manager* to manage projects successfully. All you need is a basic understanding of a few tactics, techniques, and tools, which you'll learn here.

The better you get at managing projects, the more value you bring to your boss. And for every project, you'll encounter obstacles along the way. All you need to do is to convert each obstacle into another project and make it go away.

Your effectiveness in the eyes of your boss requires that you satisfy these two conditions:

- To be able to consistently produce excellent results.

- To be able to add value to all those who help you produce those results-including your boss.

And to meet these two conditions requires that you successfully manage projects. Let's address the basics first.

What's a project?

I define a project as an assignment that requires the effort of others. Anything you can do yourself is a task and not a project. So whenever you get stuck at work, realize there's a simple way to re-frame anything into a project to get things moving again.

What's a Plan of Action?

Every project needs a good *Plan of Action*, even if it's only a mental plan or a sketch on the back of a napkin. Any good *Plan of Action (POA)* format (Appen A) has at least six components:

Objective: Who, What, Where, When, and Why (Appen A)?

Methods: How will we accomplish this Objective (Appen A)?

Timetable: Planning backward from today, how will we use the time available to plan and prepare (Appen A and Chaps 6-7)?

Resources: What will you need (Appen A)?

Unresolved Issues: What are all the things (questions, unknowns, concerns, shortfalls, obstacles, or problems) that could slow or stop your progress (Appen. A, Chap. 16)?

Risk: What could *reasonably-go-wrong* and how can they be *mitigated* (Appen A and Chaps 24-29)?

If you don't know a specific piece of information, still list the category, but show a TBD (To Be Determined). For example, if you don't know the end time, show, End time: TBD.

What's a Project's Life Cycle?

Every project has at least four phases: Planning, Preparing (before), Executing (during), and Assessing (during).

Here's a *Gannt Chart* showing the four phases of a one-day project that begins in 30-days:

Phase	Typical Gannt Chart for a Project Starting in 30-Days.			
	1	15	25	30
1	Planning	IPR		
2		Preparing	IPR	
3			Executing	AAR
4	Assessing			

Notice that the *Assessing Phase* is conducted continuously throughout the project and is formalized using two *In-Progress Reviews* (or IPRs) (Chapter 24), numerous *Project Updates* (Chapter 18), and one *After-Action Review* (or AAR) (Chapter 32).

4

BY USING
PREVENTIVE ACTIONS

"The policy of being too cautious is the greatest risk of all."
- Jawaharlal Nehru

How do you find problems, or do you wait until they find you? Do you know how to uncover and resolve anything that could slow or stop your work?

Preventive Actions are all the things you should be doing 30, 60, or 90 days before any project to uncover all Pre-Problems.

This process is designed to find and correct any Pre-Problems before they get in front of your boss or the customer.

Pre-Problems include mistakes, defects, shortfalls, omissions, errors, or anything else that could slow or stop your work.

Here are the 20 most important *Preventive Actions* that should be added to your *Project's Timetable*.

THE PLANNING PHASE

1. Conduct an initial Site Inspection:

Visit the site to see if it meets your requirements. If you're asked to select the best site, visit several sites and present the best to your boss. Gather sufficient information (like photos, dimensions, and sketch maps) to help you create your *Draft Plan of Action* (Appendix A) and prepare for your *Backbriefing* (Chapter 12). The most important issues are location, availability, accessibility, cost, and amenities when picking the best site.

2. Create a Draft Plan of Action (POA):

This is your project *Plan of Action* (POA) that includes an Objective, Methods, Risk, Timetable, Resources Needed, and Unresolved Issues. (Appendix A).

3. Identify and eliminate all Unresolved Issues:

What are all the questions, unknowns, concerns, shortfalls, obstacles, or problems that could slow or stop our progress (Chapter 21)? Each issue can only be eliminated when it's both *"known for certain"* and *"acceptable to you."*

4. Anticipate the Unintended Consequences:

What are all the adverse outcomes that aren't expected by your actions (Chapter 22)? Work hard to find anyone who has done this or a similar project before. What problems, consequences, and effects did they have?

5. Anticipate the Second and Third-Order Effects:

What are all the ways your project could affect others at different levels in your company (Chapter 22)? Work hard to find anyone who has done this or a similar project before. What problems, consequences, and effects did they have?

6. Conduct a Risk Assessment:

With your team's help, assess the risk of any safety, security, financial, and operational risk associated with the project and how they can be mitigated (Chapter 27).

7. Conduct a Backbriefing:

This is a briefing given by the Project Manager to his boss explaining how he intends to accomplish his boss's objective. This briefing enhances mutual understanding and trust by exchanging questions and answers to identify unmet expectations or hidden surprises (Chapter 12). Brief your boss using the *Plan of Action Checklist* (Appendix A). Then, set the schedule for periodic *Project Updates* (Chapter 18).

8. Create a Memorandum of Record:

Finally, create a memo documenting the questions and answers from the *Backbriefing* and any questions you couldn't answer. Ensure your boss and all Key Players get a copy. A Key Player is anyone who must perform a task for a project to achieve its objective.

9. Provide Advanced Warning:

This is informing all Key Players of what's coming, so they can plan. Provide a copy of your Draft POA and the memo from the *Backbriefing* to each Key Player (Chapter 13).

10. Create Contingency Plans:

This plan is executed only if something bad happens that was anticipated, like bad weather (Chapter 30).

11. Staff the POA:

Circulate your POA through all Key Players for their concurrence or non-concurrence with comments (Chapter 23)

Conduct a Decision Briefing: Optional

Conduct a final briefing to the Decision Maker, with all Key Players present, to obtain final approval, if needed (Appendix C).

12. Conduct In-Progress Review (IPR 1):

Conduct at least two meetings before your project to synchronize all Key Players (Chapter 24). IPR 1 should be conducted at the mid-point of the time remaining between the Planning and Preparation Phases.

THE PREPARATION PHASE

13. Conduct Project Update Briefings:

Conduct a briefing to your boss summarizing the status of your project (Chapter 18). Or you could give your boss a *Situation Report* (Chapter 19).

14. Prepare to take Immediate Action:

This is a disciplined drill used to react to bad situations that could cause a work stoppage, property or equipment damage, a security breach, or physical injury (Appendix B).

15. Conduct a Final Site Inspection:

Conduct a last inspection of the project site to see if anything has changed since the initial inspection.

16. Conduct In-Progress Review (IPR 2):

This is a second (or final) meeting conducted 5 to 7-days before the project to confirm that all assigned tasks have been completed as planned (Chapter 24) between the Preparation and Execution Phases. This is when the rehearsal schedule should be distributed.

THE EXECUTION PHASE

17. Conduct Rehearsals:

This is your last chance to see, practice, or test everything before the project to identify and correct any *Pre-Problems* (Chapter 31).

18. Conduct Pre-Staging:

This is the storage of equipment and supplies at the site before a project to make setup easier.

19. Conduct Site Set up:

Set up your site as planned. Having a site diagram (with extra copies) is a good idea – showing where everything goes.

Project Starts:

Supervise all Key Players to ensure the project achieves the desired objective. If problems arise, either execute *Immediate Action* (Appendix B) or a *Contingency Plan* (Chapter 31) to keep the project moving.

Conduct Site Clearing:

This includes all the actions taken after a project. The site may need to be cleared quickly to allow the next user to come in and stage their equipment.

THE ASSESSING PHASE

The Assessing Phase is conducted continuously throughout the project. It's formalized using at least two *In-Progress Reviews* (or IPRs), several Project Updates, and an *After-Action Review* (or AAR).

20. Conduct an After-Action Review (AAR):

Conduct an informal meeting at the end of every project day and the day after the project with all Key Players present to focus on what happened vs. what was supposed to happen. Ask, *"What did we learn that can make us better next time?"* Add the *Lessons Learned* to the *After-Action Report* (Chapter 33).

Conduct Project Close-out:

This includes all close-out details, like administering surveys, paying bills, sending letters, filing the *After-Action Report*, and other details.

5
BY USING A
PROJECT TIMETABLE

Time and tide wait for no man."
- Geoffrey Chaucer

Do you know how to create a *Project Timetable* for your next project to ensure you've identified all important tasks, their proper sequence, and who's responsible for each? Your *Project's Timetable* should also contain all the *Preventive Actions* you'll need to manage your project.

Here's an example of a partial project timetable.

Partial Timetable for Company Picnic (June 21)							
Yr	M	D	Time	Preventive Action	Responsible	Where	Who
14	5	2	1 PM	Site visit conducted	Bob	B	1
14	5	4	2 PM	Backbriefing	Bob	A	2

Notice that this table shows the date, time, the *Preventive Action*, the person responsible, the location, who else is involved, and the correct sequence for each action.

The sequence is important because **Murphy's Law on Sequence** states:

> **"Whenever attempting to do anything, there are
> always things you should have done first."**

What did you forget (Appendix E)?

Which *Preventive Actions* will you add to your *Project's Timetable* to catch all the *Pre-Problems* before your project starts?

What if you don't know the dates yet?

Here's an example:

> *Bob was having lunch with Joe (one of his Direct Reports) and asked about an important project for his boss. Joe said, "I'll start working on the POA when the company decides on a start date." Bob asked him why he was waiting. Joe responded, "How can I write a POA when I don't know when the project starts?"*

*Bob was stunned! He told Joe that the project starts every year in April, and today was January 1ˢᵗ, so he only had three months to plan. After lunch, Bob guided him through the creation of a Timetable using **S-Day as the Start Date**. Bob also asked Joe to add the most appropriate Preventive Actions to his Timetable.*

Here's an example of Joe's partial *Timetable*.

Partial Timetable for _____ Project (as of Date)							
Yr.	M	D	Time	Preventive Actions	Responsible	Where	Who
15	4	S-7	TBA	Final IPR	Joe	A	2
15	4	S-2	TBA	Rehearsals	Joe	A	2
15	4	S-1	TBA	Equipment pre-staged	Sam	B	2
15	4	S-Day	TBA	Project Starts	Joe	B	1
15	4	S+1	TBA	After Action Review	Joe	A	2

Notice that this timetable uses **S-Dates** instead of calendar dates because the project's start date has not yet been announced.

Joe then created a POA around this Timetable and began the Planning Phase. He labeled anything in the POA he didn't know for sure as TBA: To Be Announced. He then provided Advance Warning to all Key Players by giving them a copy of his draft POA. When the actual start day was announced, he plugged in the dates, notified all Key Players, and continued the Preparation Phase. If Joe had waited until the date was announced, several Key Players would have been in the last-minute crisis management mode.

Note: In the absence of instructions, make the assumptions needed to move the work forward (Appendix D).

If you fail to include *Preventive Actions* in your *Project's Timetable*, expect to experience the adverse effects of *Murphy's Law*.

6
BY USING AN
ASSESSMENT SYSTEM

*"Don't tell your problems to people: eighty percent don't care;
and the other twenty percent are glad you have them."*
- Lou Holtz

How do you find problems, or do you wait for them to find you?

**An Assessment System is a combination of targeted,
proactive procedures designed to identify problems before
they occur and resolve problems once identified.**

This system is called CAPA (Corrective Actions, Preventive Actions) and
should be part of your overall Quality Management System (QMS) and
includes procedures to prevent problems (PA) and procedures to correct
problems (CA) once identified.

*Mistakes or defects are not a problem if they're identified
and resolved before your boss or customer discovers them.*

By using Preventive Actions

**Preventive Actions are a series of specific
procedures designed to identify pre-problems before
they get in front of your boss or the customer?**

Pre-problems include anything that could slow or stop the achievement of
your goals (Chapter 4). What procedures do you have to identify problems
BEFORE they get in front of your boss or the customer?

- Do you have processes, procedures, tests, rehearsals, inspections, visits, or assessments?
- Do you need periodic inspections, rehearsals, visits, or assessments to catch defects and mistakes?
- Who's checking, and what are they checking for?
- How often and to whom do they report?
- What do they do when a problem is identified?

- Who's checking the checker?

By taking Corrective Action

Corrective Actions are a series of specific procedures designed to respond to problems AFTER they've been identified.

What procedures do you have to correct problems after they have been identified?

What's the Essence of a Finding?

Here's a system to capture, track, and resolve problems:

- **Problem #2214:** for tracking.
- **Standard:** What is the standard?
- **Condition:** What problem was found or observed?
- **Cause:** What is the root cause of this problem?
- **Risk:** What's our Risk?
    - ✓ *Impact:* How <u>serious</u> will this problem affect the project?
    - ✓ *Probability:* How <u>likely</u> is this problem to happen?
- **Recommendation:** What needs to be done to mitigate or eliminate the root cause?
- **Action:**
    - ✓ Who is the *Point of Contact (POC)* to find a solution?
    - ✓ When and how is the report rendered?
    - ✓ What is being done to correct the problem?
    - ✓ What is the current situation – same or worse and why?

Remember, mistakes or defects are not a problem if they're resolved before your boss or customer discovers them.

What do sports teams use?

The day after the game, they all watch the game video. They document and record what happened. Then, they review the entire game, play by play. Did each play accomplish its goal? Did every team member do their job? If not, what needs to be done to improve for the next game?

Here are the most effective systems to prevent and correct problems.

Corrective Actions/Preventive Actions (CAPA) part of the Quality Management Program (QMP).		
TYPE	PREVENTIVE SYSTEMS	CORRECTIVE SYSTEMS
Purpose	To identify Pre-Problems BEFORE they get in front of the boss or client.	To respond to problems AFTER being identified to resolve or mitigate their effects.
Meeting	In-Process Review, Backbriefing, Rehearse, Practice, Testing, Build consensus, Consequences and Effects, Decision Matrix, Decision Support Tools, Common-Sense Test.	After-Action Review (AAR), Essence of a Finding, Video tape review, Eisenhower Matrix.
Procedure	Follow up, Risk Assessment, Metrics, OKR, KPI, BOE, Decision Points, Decision Matrix, Red Team-Blue Team.	Immediate Action, Decision Support Templates, Sensitivity Analysis.
Reports	Unresolved Issues, Project Updates, Follow-through	Project Update Briefing, Project Dashboard, Unresolved.Issues.
Document	Plan of Action, Preventive Actions, Timetable, Unanticipated Situation Plan	Contingency Plan, Mitigation Plan, Unanticipated Situation Plan.
Observe	Checking, Inspections, visits, and Intuition	Surveys, Video tape review

This should be included as part of your Quality Management Program (QMP).

This page is intentionally left blank.

7
BY UNCOVERING
ALL EXPECTATIONS

"Exceed your customer's expectations. If you do, they'll come back over and over. Give them what they want - and a little more."
- Sam Walton.

The fact remains that you could be the most talented person on the planet, but if you don't understand and meet all the expectations of your boss, company, and industry, you're doomed to failure.

An expectation is a belief that's centered on the future.

A less than expected result gives rise to the emotion of disappointment. If something happens that's not expected, it causes the emotion of surprise. And trust me when I say bosses don't like surprises. Expectations focus on the desired performance for both results and behavior. To become more effective, you must understand all that's expected of you.

Here are the three most important expectations in the workforce:

By identifying All Stated Expectations

Stated expectations are verbal expectations from your boss and written expectations from the company found in your job description and company policies and procedures.

Here are the most important steps to identify all your stated or written expectations:

1. Know your duties.

Your duties are the tasks your boss needs you to perform and are normally found in your job description.

2. Know your responsibilities.

Responsibility is an obligation to satisfactorily perform a task assigned by your boss, which has a penalty for failure and should be in your job description. Accepting complete responsibility for what you say and do (and what you fail to say and do) and the consequences are the first step on the path to peak performance and effectiveness.

> ## What's the difference between Duty and Responsibility?
> *"Duties can be assigned and reassigned, but responsibilities can't!"*

3. Know your Constraints.

Constraints include imperatives and restrictions.

- **Imperatives** are things you must do (like achieving your goals).

- **Restrictions** are things you must not do (like not accepting gifts from vendors) and include borders and limits.

  - ✓ **Borders** are official or unofficial lines dividing one area from another, showing who's responsible for what.

  - ✓ **Limits** are the point at which something ends or beyond which something starts.

4. Know your level of Authority.

Authority is your boss's permission to take specific agreed-upon actions on her behalf in support of your official duties and responsibilities.

Authority, unlike responsibility, can be given to another person to perform a specific assignment. When you ask someone to perform an assignment, you're giving that person your authority to act on your behalf. Authority can include making work assignments, hiring and firing, making decisions, or spending money.

So, when you ask someone to perform an assignment, be clear on what they can and cannot do. Also, do you have the authority you need to perform your duties and responsibilities? If not, speak up!

5. Know your Projects.

Do you know all the past projects completed before you arrived, your ongoing projects, and your future projects coming up soon? A project is any assignment that requires the effort of others, like an activity or event.

6. Know the Standards.

Standards are the established norm or required minimum level of conformity to industry and company policy, criteria, methods, processes, and practices for your results and behavior.

To find the standards that apply to you, review all company guidelines, policies, standards of conduct, and behavior, along with any Standard Operating Procedures. Pay particular attention to safety, security, proprietary information, and intellectual property. This is especially important if you're changing jobs or getting a new boss.

By identifying All Inherent Expectations

If you're responsible for the performance of others, you have another type of duty or expectation.

**Inherent duties are boss only duties expected
and performed by all bosses that cannot be reassigned.**

Here are the most important boss-only inherent duties or expectations that will consume 90% of the boss's time:

- Traveling and attending meetings he must attend.

- Conducting internal meetings and following-through.

- Briefings those he must brief.

- Responding to emails, voicemails, and other correspondence.

- Delegating actions and problems to team members to resolve.

- *Training members on how to complete projects.

- Solving problems only he can resolve.

- Conducting interviews, checking, and inspecting.

- Planning, organizing, building teams, training, delegating, and setting goals and priorities.

- Enforcing standards, correcting, counseling, reprimanding, retraining, and punishing.

- Inspiring, motivating, praising, encouraging, consoling, challenging, coaching, and promoting.

As you consider these *boss-only inherent duties*, realize they're the most important things every boss must do.

*To learn more about *Training*, available at **Amazon.com,** see page 5.

Hidden expectations are things that others expect you to do that are either unclear, unspoken, or unwritten.

These expectations are the most dangerous because they lead to poor performance, mistakes, and failure (Chapter 37).

For any boss to have faith in you, the issue always involves your performance (your results and behavior).

- Your **results** involve your ability to consistently produce excellent results.

- Your **behavior** involves how well you add value to all those who helped you achieve your results, especially your boss.

If your boss's expectations are hidden or unclear, your performance will suffer along with your credibility, job security, and career. Meeting all your boss's expectations will put you way ahead of your peers.

Here are the most important steps to uncover hidden expectations.

Step 1. Assume nothin!

Be careful with your assumptions (Appendix D).

Step 2. Meet with your boss and ask these questions:

- What's your mission, intent, purpose, and direction?
- What're your goals, values, focus, and priorities?
- What're your expectations of me at your meetings?
- What reports or updates do you expect from me?
- How will you assess my performance for both results and behavior?
- Do I have permission to voice my honest opinion, behind closed doors, without the fear of negative consequences?
- What're your expectations of me for tradition and culture?
- Do I have access to information sharing and processing?
- What're my goals, and how do they relate to yours?
- What's my level of Authority? Does it include making work assignments, hiring, firing, making decisions, or spending money?

- What're my Imperatives (things I must do) and Restrictions (things I must not do)?

- What're my ongoing projects, and which is most important and why?

- What're my future projects, and which is most important and why?

- What are all the recurring events or activities that occur weekly, monthly, quarterly, or annually?

Step 3. Ask your team members and peers.

Ask them for any hidden expectations. Ask about your boss's idiosyncrasies, strengths, and weaknesses.

Step 4. Ask your predecessor.

Ask about any hidden or unstated expectations.

Step 5. Ask Human Resources.

Ask about any hidden or unstated expectations for culture and tradition.

This page is intentionally left blank.

8
BY CONTRIBUTING TO
THE BOSS'S MEETINGS

"It is the responsibility of leadership to provide opportunity,
and the responsibility of individuals to contribute.
- William Pollard

Do you know what you need to do and not do during your boss's meetings because this may be the only contact your boss has to observe your performance? These meetings will be attended by your boss's other Direct Reports - your Peers. So, get to know them. Help them in any way you can.

Why do bosses conduct meetings?

- To learn what's going on concerning the status of assigned work.
- To pass on what he knows about what's important to his boss.
- To monitor the team's efforts to move the work forward.

What are the most important things to do during these meetings?

- Arrive 15 minutes early to get to know your Peers.
- Display respect and kindness.
- Demonstrate support for your boss by your 100% attention, involvement, and participation.
- Put your cell phone on vibrate or leave it outside.
- Support for your peers. Teamwork is critical.
- Come with the attitude to contribute, encourage, and help others.
- Demonstrate an understanding of your boss's goals.
- If you cannot attend, send someone to discuss your agenda items and *Unresolved Issues* (Chapter 21).
- And if you have no one to send, call your boss the day before and provide your update.
- To wait for others to finish before speaking.
- To follow up with answers to questions you couldn't answer.

What are the most important things not to do during these meetings?

- Hog the air-time. Be brief and let others speak.
- Wander off the agenda. Help your boss keep others on track.
- Surprise your boss. Bosses hate surprises - unless it's great news.
- Interrupt or cut someone off. If you must, then apologize!
- Embarrass or surprise a peer.
- Find fault or complain. Only do so privately with your boss.
- Continue arguing after the boss has made his decision?
- Ask a question that could embarrass someone. Ask it privately.
- Be late or absent without calling.

If you fail to understand and meet these expectations, you'll never be considered a *Team Player*.

What's the bottom-line on Communicating?

Good communication isn't about you - it's about them.

Do they understand what you want them to do? And how do you know for sure? You won't unless you ask! And whose responsible and accountable if they don't understand and the project goes bad?

To be considered effective or essential by any boss, you must be perceived as someone who can be counted on to excel at two things:

- To consistently produce excellent results.
- To add value to all those who helped produce those results, especially the boss.

Your ability to communicate will play a huge role in that assessment.

Get your act together, or your credibility will suffer!

9
BY GIVING AND
RECEIVING FEEDBACK

"Feedback is the Breakfast of Champions"
- Ken Blanchard

Do you know how to give and receive feedback to enhance your effectiveness and the effectiveness of those with whom you work?

Feedback is information about a member's performance, which is used as a basis for improvement.

The goal of feedback is to identify the gap between <u>desired</u> and <u>actual</u> performance (for results and behavior) of members, teams, units, and systems) and to close the gap ASAP.

If you don't receive feedback, ask for it, not only from your boss but others.

Feedback can occur anytime but normally comes during audits, performance-oriented training, performance appraisals and reviews, shareholders' meetings, marketing research, 360-degree feedback, peak performance coaching, visits and observations, on-site inspections, surveys, meetings, and *After-Action Reviews.*

What's the Feedback Loop for Human Performance?

Here are the most important steps of the *Feedback Loop.*

Step 1: Evidence: The performance must be measured, recorded, and assessed.

Step 2: Relevance: Feedback must be relayed to the member in a context that makes sense.

Step 3: Consequence: Feedback must illuminate a path to improvement.

Step 4: Action: Members must change their <u>actual</u> performance to come closer to the <u>desired</u> performance.

Then, that new performance can be re-measured, and the feedback loop can run once more, every action stimulating new performance that moves the member closer to the <u>desired</u> performance.

How do you give Feedback?

If you fail to provide periodic and specific feedback to your members, your silence will speak louder than words. It's your job to let them know how they're doing.

- If your feedback is **positive,** share it with everyone publicly.

- If your feedback is **negative** or a correction (like someone failed to meet a standard), do so privately. Take a moment to ensure the member knew the correct standard and didn't have a good reason for doing (or failing to do) what he did.

However, giving someone your opinion doesn't constitute feedback unless they act on your opinion and thus cause you to revise your opinion.

How do you receive Feedback?

When you receive feedback, you get to decide how you'll respond and if you'll use it to become more effective. Feedback is often perceived as a euphemism for criticism. If you just "blow it off," you'll never get any better. You don't have to agree. Initially, you won't. However, arguing or being defensive sends the wrong message.

Humble yourself! Remember, no matter how painful, you need the feedback because you'll never become more effective or successful without it. Also, the person giving the feedback might someday be in a position to shape your future. So, be *self-correcting*! Prove that you're listening and getting better every day (Appendix G).

Effective people thrive on feedback because their goal is to become more effective and successful.

10

BY PROVIDING
FEEDBACK TO THE BOSS

"If I had to reduce the responsibilities of a good follower
to a single rule, it would be to speak truth to power. "
- Warren Bennis.

Do you know how to provide meaningful feedback to your boss?

Is it your job to provide feedback to your boss? Absolutely! You owe it to your boss. But how do you do it?

Providing feedback to your boss takes moral
courage and is the most challenging part of being loyal to
your boss; telling him what he doesn't want to hear
- like the TRUTH.

Feedback is normally defined as information that you privately provide to someone intended to improve their performance. However, when it comes to your boss, it's a little more complicated. When providing feedback to your boss, your intent must be perceived as being done to help him stay out of trouble, avoid or correct a mistake, resolve problems, achieve his goals, and look good in the eyes of his boss. As such, here are the most important steps:

Step 1. Set the stage.

This means that whatever you have to say must be done privately. You might even suggest that you and your boss take a walk to somewhere private where you won't be interrupted.

Step 2. Gain permission.

If you've not already done so, ask and receive confirmation that you have permission to be honest.

Step 3. Preface your remarks.

Preface your remarks by saying, *"I need to give you some feedback on..."* or *"I just wanted to tell you how I feel about...."* or *"I just thought you needed to know..."*

Step 4. Deliver your message.

Speak your peace and remind your boss of why you're saying what you did.

- **What happens if your boss gets angry?** This could happen - no big deal. You're not there to blow smoke up his butt. You're there to make him and his unit better tomorrow than they are today. Period!

- **What if I get fired?** My response is, Great! You're the lucky one! You no longer have to work for a jerk who fails to appreciate your loyalty for telling the truth.

Privately providing honest feedback to your boss is the stronger half of courage and loyalty.

When was the last time you took your boss for a walk and discussed what was going on?

Caution: There is a fine line between tattling and reporting the facts. Tattling is done to get someone in trouble. Feedback is done to either keep him out of trouble, help him achieve his goals, or to make him look good in the eyes of his boss. When you tell your boss about a mistake he made or is about to make, you're doing so to keep him out of trouble. Do you have good communication with your boss? If not, why? If in doubt, ask!

Remember, the only stupid question is the one you're too afraid to ask. Because, later, when you don't know the answer, you will look stupid or worse!

Note: As a new member, during your first 90-days, you can ask any question you want, and no one will care. After that, they'll be wondering why they hired you!

11
BY
TAKING-CHARGE

When in doubt, mumble; when in trouble,
delegate; when in charge, ponder.
- James H. Boren

This chapter assumes that your boss has assigned you a project, and you're in the process of *taking-charge* as the Project Manager (PM).

Important Terms and Concepts

Backbriefing:

A briefing given by the Project Manager (PM) to his boss BEFORE starting a project, explaining how the PM intends to accomplish the boss's objective.

Being in-charge:

This means that you're the boss of a project (an assignment that requires the effort of others) assigned by your boss. Sometimes, your boss will make you the coordinator for a project. It could also be called the lead, point person, or facilitator. These are all ways of saying that you're *in-charge* with limitations.

When in-charge, take-charge!

Only your boss can tell you the extent of those limitations. If in doubt, ask! Make no assumptions. Do you have the authority to make decisions, task others, assign work, hire, fire, spend money, and set priorities? This is why you should always conduct a *Backbriefing* with your boss.

Boss:

The person you report to for your work assignments and pays you for your products and services.

Briefback:

A question and answer meeting called by the PM to ensure all participants understand the Plan of Action, their duties and responsibilities, consequences and effects, unresolved issues, and what to do when things go wrong.

Flexibility to Respond:

As the PM, you represent your boss in everything you do to ensure the project's success. However, you must retain your *Flexibility to Respond* because plans and projects rarely unfold as expected.

**Flexibility to Respond is your Freedom of Action
to check on your project, resolve problems, and remain
responsive to your members and your boss.**

This means always staying in contact with all participants and your boss, being free to roam and reposition your members, equipment, or supplies to where they're most needed. That means that you must delegate any problems or obstacles to another team member or Key Play so that you don't get diverted with ancillary issues causing you to take your eye off the big picture. Once you get bogged down as a doer, you're no longer the PM.

Effective PMs are in-motion checking and encouraging!

Key Player:

Anyone who must perform a task for your project to succeed and doesn't report to you (like a vendor, supplier, or a member of a different department).

Project:

Any assignment that requires the effort of others to achieve the objective and includes achieving goals, resolving problems, and conducting activities or events.

Project Manager:

The person assigned by the boss to conduct a project: the *person-in-charge.*

Tasking Authority:

Your ability to assign work to another member. For example, you only have *tasking authority* over your direct reports, which are those members who report to you for their work assignments. If they don't work for you, you have no *tasking authority*. However, your boss and his boss have *tasking authority* over many more members that can be assigned to you temporally to complete your project.

Team Member:

This includes anyone who normally reports to you for their work assignments, your Direct Reports.

By knowing what a PM does

When In-Charge, Take-Charge!

What are the most important things a PM should do?

- Always protect your *Flexibility to Respond*.

- Step up and take responsibility and accountability for a project from start to finish (Appendix G).

- Ask questions, listen to concerns, pay attention, and delegate authority, but never responsibility.

- Build consensus with the team.

- Facilitate problem-solving and collaboration.

- Be willing to change the plan when needed, demonstrate flexibility, and adapt to changing conditions.

- When things go wrong, you own the mistakes. When things go well, you share the success.

- Be proactive and responsive by checking and making things happen!

- Provide a Backbriefing to your boss to ensure you understand his expectations.

What should a PM NOT do?

As the PM, you should NOT:

- Become engaged in physically helping a team member because it limits your *Flexibility to Respond* elsewhere.

- Attempt to resolve problems or unresolved issues. Delegate it to a team member.

Here's a Great Story:

One day, John (the boss) visited a work site to check on a sub-project conducted by one of his Direct Reports (Bob). John asked Bob how things were going. Bob had two job sites as part of his sub-project.

John then visited Bob's second job site and saw that the members there were doing nothing. Bob's members tried to call Bob but got no answer. John tried to call Bob but got no response. Frustrated, John drove back to the first site and asked Bob why he wasn't answering his phone. Bob said his phone was in his truck.

John then pulled Bob aside for some on-the-job correcting and said, "Bob, I need you to have your phone with you at all times. Also, I just came from your second site and found that your team had no idea what they were supposed to do. I need you to get over there to straighten things out. Also, you need to check both your sites first thing every morning to ensure they get started the right way.

Bob lost his *Flexibility to Respond* because he left his phone in his truck, and no one could contact him.

Are you a Micro-Manager?

Well, let's see. The opposite of effective delegation is micromanagement.

Micromanagement is a management style whereby the boss closely observes and controls the work of a Direct Report.

Micromanagement also includes the suppression of constructive criticism that could otherwise lead to internal reform and job turnover. In micromanagement, the boss not only tells the Direct Report WHAT to do but dictates HOW to do it.

So, are you a micro-manager? Do you trust your Direct Reports? Would they agree? Any room for improvement?

12
BY CONDUCTING A
BACKBRIEFING

"Progress always involves risks. You can't steal
second base and keep your foot on first."
- Frederick B. Wilcox

This chapter assumes that your boss's assigned you as the Project Manager (PM) for an upcoming project. One way to ensure no unmet expectations and misunderstandings between you and your boss before your next project is to conduct a Backbriefing.

A Backbriefing is a briefing given by the Project Manager to his boss BEFORE starting a project, explaining how the PM intends to accomplish the boss's objective.

As far as your boss is concerned, if he assigned you to be the *person-in-charge* of an assignment - the assignment belongs to you – and you're the Project Manager. Backbriefings are an excellent way to achieve a "meeting of the minds" before work begins. They enhance mutual understanding and trust by exchanging questions and answers to ensure no unmet expectations or hidden surprises later. They benefit all parties by reducing misunderstandings and the need for rework. They also enhance your credibility, thus relieving the need for micromanagement.

When should a Backbriefing be conducted?

There are two types of projects in business: **Expected Projects** are projects already part of your job description, like an annual trade show. For expected projects, provide a Backbriefing at least 90 days before the project. And **Requested Projects** are newly assigned projects and should receive a Backbriefing a week after receiving the assignment.

Here are the most important steps to conduct a good Backbriefing:

Step 1. Conduct an Initial Site Inspection.

Visit the site to see if it meets the requirements. If you're asked to select the best site, visit several sites and present the best to your boss. Gather sufficient information (like photos, dimensions, and sketch maps) to help you create your Draft Plan of Action (Appendix A) and prepare for your Backbriefing (Chapter 12).

The most important issues when picking the best site are location, availability, accessibility, and cost.

Step 2. Create your Draft Plan of Action.

Use the Plan of Action Checklist in (Appendix A) to create your draft.

Step 3. Identify and eliminate all Unresolved Issues.

An Unresolved Issue is any question, unknown, concern, shortfall, obstacle, or problem that could slow or stop your progress (Chapter 21).

Step 4. Anticipate the Consequences and Effects.

List any Unintended Consequences and Second and Third-Order Effects (Chapter 22). Find someone who has done this or a similar work before. What problems, consequences, and effects did they have?

Step 5. Conduct a Risk Assessment.

Assess the risk of anything that could slow or stop your project or cause physical harm, security failures, and financial loss and how they can be mitigated (Chapter 27).

Step 6. Brief your boss using the Plan of Action Checklist (Appendix A).

You're not expected to have all the answers, but you're expected to have all the questions. So, as a minimum, obtain answers to these questions:

- What's the desired end-result or objective?
- How will success be measured?
- What are all the most important tasks that must be completed?
- Who's responsible for each major task?
- What's your authority to make decisions and spend money?

Then, set the schedule for periodic Project Updates (Chapter 18). Capture any new Unresolved Issues or questions your boss asked that you couldn't answer. If the boss doesn't want a Backbriefing, send him your draft POA and get his approval.

Step 7. Create a Memorandum of Record.

Finally, create a memo documenting what happened during the Backbriefing and any questions you couldn't answer. Ensure your boss and all Key Players get a copy. If you fail to conduct a Backbriefing with your boss before your next project, do so at your peril.

You've been WARNED!

13
BY PROVIDING
ADVANCED WARNING

"History is a vast early warning system."
- Norman Cousins

Do you know how to provide important information to your team members and Key Players to ensure they know what you're planning and have sufficient time to prepare?

How would you feel if your boss just told you that you're flying to Europe tomorrow when he's known about it for a month?

Advanced Warning is the process of informing all Key Players and team members of what you're planning, so they have sufficient time to plan.

The most important thing you can do for your team members and Key Players is to give them as much time as possible to plan and prepare by telling them what you're planning to do. You do this by providing as much Advanced Warning as you can.

In the **US Military**, it's called a *"Warning Order,"* It includes an Objective statement from the Draft *Plan of Action* (POA) telling as many specifics as possible. It should have the who, what, when, where, and why of what you're planning. Unless the task is time-sensitive, an email to each team member and Key Player should suffice. However, provide as much information as you can. If anything is unknown, list it as TBA (To Be Announced).

What's the "One-Third, Two-Thirds Rule?"

When planning a project, the rule states that if there are three weeks until a project starts, the first week is yours to create the Plan of Action and Backbrief your boss, and the two remaining weeks belong to your Key Players for their *planning and preparation.

*To learn more about **Planning**, available at **Amazon.com,** see page 5.

This page is intentionally left blank.

14
BY ACCEPTING
ASSIGNMENTS

"Success is no accident. It is hard work, perseverance, learning, studying, sacrifice and most of all, love of what you are doing or learning to do."
- Pele

When you "accept" an assignment in the workplace, this starts the Planning Phase of the Project Process. *Accepting* an assignment means you've been asked by someone (normally your boss) to do something (task or project), and you *accepted*.

Do you have to accept every assignment from your boss?

Actually, *No.* You have five options. However, if you *accept* the assignment and don't say anything, you just made a promise to deliver. This promise to deliver also includes when you tell someone you'll do something when you're asked for help, and you say you'll help. If you're not going to help, then say so! Keep your word, especially to yourself, or don't make the promise in the first place.

Whether you promise a friend, associate, your boss, a total stranger, or yourself that you'll do something by a specific time, you've already created a debt. And if you're poor at keeping your promises, this will destroy your integrity. The toxic effect of this debt is catastrophic to your relationships, as well as your self-image. If it's a bad habit, own up to it and make the change. Do you deliver on what you said you'd do? If you tell someone, *"I'll get back to you,"* do you?

Your greatest personal power is your word. Always under-promise and over-deliver! The person doing the asking could be a superior (your boss in most cases), or it could be a peer or even a subordinate. Just because someone asks you to do something doesn't mean you must *accept*.

Here are the five options you have when asked to do anything:

- **If you accept**, you begin the process of receiving the project. Accepting a project means you've been selected by someone (normally your boss) to be *in charge* of making something (the project) happen, and you agreed to accept.

Don't accept if you cannot deliver. Stop and think. If you have any concerns or reservations, say so. When you first receive a project, you must identify two things: what needs to be done and the deadline? Be careful not to accept too much, which will burn you out. Accepting too much and being afraid or too proud to say NO or ask for help is a recipe for disaster. If you intend to remain effective over the long haul, ensure you know your workload.

Part of being effective is knowing when to say NO and when to ask for HELP.

- **If you accept with conditions**, state your reasons and negotiate the conditions. Negotiating is the most underrated skill a person can have and one of the most productive. When you consider that most human communication is some form of negotiating, you'll quickly come to realize how important this skill is to your ability to influence others. Can you say NO to your boss? Of course, just make sure you have a good reason. Now the negotiations begin.

- **If you delay** by telling someone you'll get back to them, do you? Remember, your integrity is being tested here. Keep your word.

- **If you redirect**, ensure you direct them to someone (or somewhere) that can help them. Helping others builds relationships. If you can't help them or they can help themselves, direct them to the solution. Be helpful.

- **If you reject,** ensure you have a good reason. Can you reject your boss? Sure, but he'll need a good reason. Also, be prepared to negotiate because your boss may have no other choice. Be assertive and tell your boss specifically what you need, along with the consequences and effects of what won't get done.

If you ever feel you can't accomplish the objective, tell your boss immediately. He will need to provide additional resources to arrive at a *workable* solution.

15
BY NEGOTIATING
ASSIGNMENTS

"You do not get what you want. You get what you negotiate."
- Harvey Mackay

Do you have the time and other resources needed to accomplish your projects? What is the requirement and scope (complexity) of your projects?

If you have any doubt about completing a project, it's time to negotiate, and here are some things to consider.

1. Put yourself in the position of your boss.

What objections do you expect? What response do you have to these objections? Many people are afraid or too proud to negotiate and ask for help. Just by asking for something, you have a 66% chance of getting something. Every time you ask for something, your boss can say *YES*, *NO*, or he can *split the difference*. The better you negotiate, the more you'll receive.

2. Know the difference between a need and a want.

What you *need* is far more important than what you *want*. Be more assertive. Tell your boss, *"I need ... "*, and then justify it.

The stronger your Justification - the higher your Probability of Success.

And, if you get turned down, bring out all the negative effects (consequences) that could occur.

3. Increase your Leverage and Justification.

Leverage is the power you have when your boss really needs you to do something quickly.

The more your boss wants something done, the more *leverage* you have. The more *leverage* you have, the greater the probability your request will be granted.

Accepting a project is a negotiation. Your boss wants to get going on the project. If you need something, the time to ask is before you accept the project. If you wait and ask later, your *leverage* is gone.

The only power you have left is *justification.*

Justification is the compelling reason you're asking.

Here are the most important things you can do to increase your justification:

- Link your request to helping the Organization or Unit.

> **Example: "I need this new technology because it will help the company dramatically increase the quality of what we produce."**

- Link your request to achieving, maintaining, or exceeding your goals.
- Link your request to one of your boss's priorities.
- Link your request to effectiveness, efficiency, or consistency.
- Show how granting your request will make your boss look good.
- Compare yourself to someone who's already received it. (*You said Yes to Joe last week.*)
- Explain how your request is making up for something you were previously denied.
- You deserve it because you've done a great job in the past or appeal to your boss's sense of fairness.

Be prepared to justify your request and prepare a persuasive argument to address any objections presented by your boss. If turned down, be ready to present the adverse consequences.

4. Ask for more than you need.

When you ask for anything, your boss can answer in three different ways. He can say, *Yes, No, or split the difference* and give you half of what you asked for. Anticipate this.

If you're negotiating budget money for a project and want $5,000, ask for $10,000 instead. This way, your boss can think he's winning the negotiation by granting you $5,000.

16

BY MAKING
ASSIGNMENTS TO OTHERS

"When you delegate work to the member of the team, your job is to clearly frame success and describe the objectives."
- Steven Sinofsky

This chapter assumes that you have several Direct Reports.

What are the most important things to provide to your Direct Report BEFORE they start planning their projects?

- Provide a clear picture of what you want done (Direction).

- Set a deadline for completion.

- Explain why (Purpose) you need it done and its importance.

- Record it in your *Assignment Tracking Form* (Appendix F).

- State any constraints (things he must and must not do).

- Explain the extent of his authority to make decisions and spend money.

- Provide access to sources of relevant info and be available for questions or problems 24/7.

- State your expectations and how success will be measured

- Set a date for the *Backbriefing* (Chapter 12).

- Explain the format is the POA format (Appendix A)

- Ask for periodic *Project Updates* (Chapter 18), as needed

- Ask for all *Unresolved Issues List* weekly (Chapter 21).

- Ask for a copy of the POA and any changes as they occur.

- Use *Preventive Actions* (Chapter 4).

- Ask for the consequences, effects, and risks.

Ensure your Direct Report covers all the items from the *Plan of Action* (POA) Format and help him fill in the blanks.

After he tells you HOW he intends to accomplish the project's objective, resist changing the HOW without a good reason. Ensure the project's timetable includes all the pertinent *Preventive Actions*. If anything is missing from the POA, schedule another meeting until all items are complete.

What should you do DURING the Project?

- Show interest (pay attention, ask questions, ask for input, listen).

- Facilitate collaborative problem-solving via consensus building.

- Show appreciation (recognizing, thanking, and praising).

- Review status during future Project Updates (Chapter 18).

What about new problems that come up?

Delegate every new problem to a Direct Report, rather than trying to resolve it yourself. In some cases, these problems will become projects. If you get involved in solving problems yourself, you'll quickly lose your Flexibility to Respond. So, be careful!

Which Direct Report should you assign a new problem or project?

As I see it, you have three options. First, you could assign it to the Direct Report:

- Who has nothing to do?

- Whom do I trust the most?

- Whose duties most closely align with the problem or project?

I recommend the third option because it's good to keep problems, changes, and new projects with the team member whose responsibilities most closely fit. This ensures that the direct report receives the assignment with the greatest expertise, institutional knowledge, and experience.

And if your Direct Report becomes overwhelmed, assign others who are less engaged to assist temporarily. This is why you should always protect your *Flexibility to Respond.*

17
BY NEGOTIATING
ASSIGNMENTS TO OTHERS

"Any negotiation involves compromise and
no one will get everything they want."
- Nicky Morgan

Here are four techniques you can use when a Direct Report attempts to negotiate his assignments?

1. Is it a need or a want?

Fully understand your Direct Report's needs or reasons by asking probing questions. Is it truly a *need* or a *want*?

2. What's the urgency?

Ask, what will happen if his need goes unfulfilled for 30, 60, or 90-days? Based on his response, how does he know for sure?

3. Take time to think about it.

Unless it's something simple, don't decide until you've had a chance to think about it and discuss it with at least one trusted person. After you've carefully considered the advantages and disadvantages, consider the future consequences of your decision. If someone asks for an exception, and you grant it to one, you must be willing to grant it to all.

4. Be creative in your response.

You don't have to say *YES* or *NO* to a request. You could *split-the-difference* between what they want and what you're willing to give.

You could:

- Delay the granting until some future date.

- Link the granting to the completion of a project.

- Link the granting to their achieving or exceeding their goals.

- Grant the request, but with certain conditions that you specify.

This page is intentionally left blank.

18
BY CONDUCTING A
PROJECT UPDATE

"It takes half your life before you discover
life is a do-it-yourself project."
- Napoleon Hill

Do you know how to provide important information to your boss
concerning the current status of your projects to ensure he understands
your progress, changes, and *Unresolved Issues?*

A Project Update is a summary of a project provided to the boss
and all Key Players as to the current status of a project.

Your boss may have some changes or modifications to the original *Plan of*
Action. These last-minute changes are usually the things that complicate
any project. So, prepare for these changes, document them carefully, and
communicate them to all Key Players. There are two ways to provide a
Project Update, either by a Briefing or a Dashboard.

By conducting a Project Update Briefing

Here are the most important steps.

Step 1: Overall assessment.

When reporting the summary, give the *bottom-line up-front.* Then,
justify your assessment. For example, how's the assignment doing
concerning the scope, schedule, money, and people from the original
POA?

- **Positive assessments:** On-schedule, within budget, looking good,
  progressing nicely.
- **Negative assessments:** Behind-schedule, in trouble, over-budget,
  or has major problems.

Step 2: Unresolved Issues.

Present any question, unknown, concern, shortfall, obstacle, or problem
that could slow or stop your progress (Chapter 21). If new problems are
introduced, the boss will expect you to present options to resolve these
problems and recommend which option is best.

Your boss will also expect you to have already presented the problem to all Key Players for their concurrence or non-concurrence with comments (Chapter 23).

Step 3: Changes.

Present any new changes since your last briefing.

Step 4: Close.

Close by summarizing and restating any assignments made during the briefing or any Follow-through action. Confirm the date and time of the next update. Prepare a Memorandum for Record (MFR) to document what happened during the meeting.

By creating a Project Dashboard

The most popular type of business dashboard is the Google Analytics Dashboards, used on 55% of all websites, which shows the activity on a website, like visits, entry pages, bounce rate, and traffic sources.

A Dashboard is a graphic providing at-a-glance views of Key Performance Indicators (KPIs) relevant to a project's objective or a business process.

Post it where all Key Players can access it (like a shared-drive so all can check progress, 24/7). Here's an example of a Dashboard.

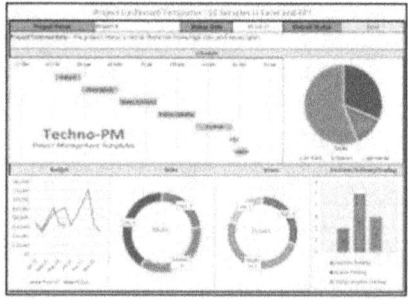

If done manually, ensure you update it every week or as changes occur. Email any changes to all concerned. Since a Dashboard is intended to provide the same material as a Project Update Briefing, design it to give the same information quickly. You can also add links to other documents, like Frequently Asked Questions (FAQ). Providing Project Updates to your boss enhances your credibility.

19
BY GIVING A
SITUATION REPORT

"Success is not built on success. It's built on failure. It's built on frustration. Sometimes it's built on catastrophe."
- Sumner Redstone

Do you know how to ensure your boss knows your workflow and unresolved issues? What do you say when your boss stops by or calls you on the phone and asks, *"What's up? What's happening"* or How's it going?"

Your boss is asking you for a *Situation Report*.

A Situation Report is a quick update to your boss stating what you're working on when you expect to finish, and any changes or unresolved issues.

If you want to stand out, give a 15-second, *Situation Report* by answering these questions:

- What are you currently working on?
- When do you expect to finish?
- What are your changes and *Unresolved Issues*?

Here's an example of a *Situation Report*:

One day, Bob took the entire day to visit all his Direct Reports at their office and asked, "What's goin on?" Most said things like, "Not much, we're okay, or same ole same-o."

However, one Direct Report said,

"I'm working on Project Alpha, which should be done by Friday. We had to change the format slightly because we couldn't get the Executive Summary to fit on one page. By the way, we still need the input from Accounting. Can you help with that?"

Bob was impressed and said, "Nice work! Thanks. I'll look into that input you need from Accounting."

When you start giving *Situation Reports* to your boss, you'll be astonished by the response.

This page is intentionally left blank.

20
BY CONDUCTING
INTERNAL MEETINGS

Murphy's Law on Meetings:
A meeting is an event at which the minutes
are kept, and the hours are lost.

Do you know how to conduct productive and meaningful meetings to enhance the quality and effectiveness of your team?

Have you ever been to a meeting that was a waste of time, and you just wanted to leave? Was it your meeting? Today, many face-to-face, sit-down meetings are often unproductive, especially when considering all the advanced communication technology available. However, meetings can be productive and meaningful, and here are a few suggestions.

1. Simplify your Agenda.

Most meetings I've attended failed to get to the heart of the problems needing attention. Here are the most important components:

- **Present:** What are you currently working on, and when do you expect to finish?

- **Future:** What are you planning to accomplish before our next meeting?

- **Unresolved Issues:** Do you have any questions, unknowns, concerns, shortfalls, obstacles, or problems that could slow or stop your progress (Chapter 21)?

After starting the meeting, go around the room and ask everyone to comment on their three agenda items. You may even request that everyone submit their three agenda items via email to you or the meeting facilitator the day before. This way, a copy of each person's response can be provided to all participants at the meeting.

2. Preside instead of conduct.

Ask someone else to conduct your meeting so that you can preside. Conducting a meeting is good training for your #2 person. It allows you to observe the body language, note who's not participating, and inject, clarifies, question, reinforce, or redirect, as needed.

---

3. Hold members accountable (Appendix G).

In a non-threatening way, *accountability* means asking:

- How are you progressing on your assignments?
- How do you intend to resolve your problems?
- Do you need more time or other resources?

If someone needs more time to complete an assignment, consider renegotiating a new deadline (Appendix F).

4. Don't get distracted.

The reason for not dealing with new, non-emergency, *Unresolved Issues* is to avoid being distracted and losing focus during your meeting.

What if a new Unresolved Issue is brought up that's a non-emergency and can't be resolved quickly?

- Assign someone to lead another meeting to resolve the issue. Assign all others that you feel need to be at that meeting.
- Assign the person who brought up the issue to write a *Decision Paper* (Appendix C).
- Assign the person who brought up the issue to come to see you with a recommended solution before the next meeting.

Most importantly, don't leave this issue without an assignment. Near the end of the meeting, review all assignments made during the meeting.

5. Consider setting these expectations.

- Meetings start and end on time and last no more than one hour.
- If you can't attend, send someone to discuss your agenda items.
- Bad language isn't permitted, and only one person speaks at a time.
- No *throwing anyone under-the-bus*, especially if not present.
- Do everything you can to support each other (Teamwork is critical).
- No distractions, no texting or communicating on any devices.
- I expect your 100% attention, involvement, and participation.
- I expect you to treat everyone with respect and kindness
- Come to participate, contribute, encourage, and help others.

21
BY ELIMINATING
UNRESOLVED ISSUES

*"There are two ways of spreading light: to be the candle
or the mirror that reflects it."*
- Edith Wharton

Do you know how to identify and eliminate any uncertainty that could stop
or slow your ability to consistently produce excellent results?

**An Unresolved Issue is any question, unknown,
concern, shortfall, obstacle, or problem that
could slow or stop your progress.**

Your mission is to hunt down and eliminate all the *Unresolved Issues*
associated with your work. If you don't, *Murphy's Law* will surely ruin
your day. Don't let this happen to you!

So, do yourself a favor. Identify and eliminate all your *Unresolved Issues*
early on to avoid the frustration, mistakes, and potential failure that could
result from not having *your-act-together.*

Here are the most important steps to eliminate all your *Unresolved Issues.*

Step 1. Identify all Issues.

To identify all your *Unresolved Issues*, seek good answers to these
questions.

- What do we need to know but don't?

- What do we know for sure, but the answer is unsatisfactory or
  unacceptable?

- What are all things we need but don't have?

- What are all the questions, unknowns, concerns, shortfalls,
  obstacles, or problems that could slow or stop your progress?

- Who has done this type of work before, and what were their
  problems, consequences, and effects?

- What are we forgetting to do (Appendix E)?

Step 2. State each issue in one sentence.

Each *Unresolved Issue* should be stated in one sentence and answer these questions.

- What do we need specifically?
- How much (or how many) do we need, exactly?
- Why do we need it - the purpose?
- When's the latest we need it?
- Where do we need it?

For example, let's assume that you're responsible for a *Team-Building Session* for your company, but you still need a guest speaker. So, your *Unresolved Issue* might read:

> *"Need to identify and contract one guest speaker for the final dinner, on June 23, at our annual Team-Building Session at the Hilton Hotel no later than June 1."*

Step 3. Add it to the Unresolved Issues List.

Here's a simple table for your *Unresolved Issues*.

Unresolved Issues List				
Date	Action Item	Who	Deadline	Status/ Date
May 4	Need to identify and contract one guest speaker for the final dinner, on June 23, at our annual Team-Building Session at the Hilton Hotel no later than June 1.	Tom	June 23	Ongoing /May 10

Notice that this table captures the date the issue was identified (May 4), the action item stated in one sentence, Tom is responsible for resolving the issue, the deadline (DL) is June 23, and the current status with the date you last checked is "Ongoing/May 10."

The reason for this much detail is to enable your boss and his boss to help you resolve your issues without asking you any questions.

Step 4. Provide a copy to your boss.

Always ensure your boss has a current copy of all your *Unresolved Issues*. If he doesn't have these details, he can't help you.

Step 5. Continue to eliminate each issue.

All *Unresolved Issues* should go on your list until two things happen:

- Until the answer is *known for certain*, means that the answer must be a fact rather than an opinion or speculation.

- Until the answer is *acceptable to you*, means that it's no longer an issue.

Keep the issue on your list until the issue is both *"Known for Certain"* and *"Acceptable to You."* Don't be surprised when one issue is resolved that several new issues appear. Just add them to your list and get as much help as you can to resolve each issue.

Step 6. Seek Assistance.

Also, discuss your *Unresolved Issues* during any future meetings or updates. Others at the meeting may be able to help you - but they need to know your issues.

Look, this technique is designed to help you get things done. No one can help you if they don't know your Unresolved Issues. So, don't let your pride or fear get in your way.

Always remember,

Asking for help is a sign of strength, not a sign of weakness.

Not knowing you need help is a sign of ignorance.

And needing help and not asking for it is a sign of stupidity.

So, don't get stuck on stupid!

When an issue is resolved, don't delete it from your list because you'll need it later for your *After-Action Review* (Chapter 32). Just record it as completed. Also, notify your boss.

Remember, the worst thing you could ever do is to conceal your Unresolved Issues from your boss.

This page is intentionally left blank.

22

BY ANTICIPATING
CONSEQUENCES AND EFFECTS

"The world is moved not only by the mighty shoves of heroes, but also by the aggregate of the tiny pushes of each honest worker."
- Helen Keller

Do you know how to anticipate and mitigate things that could produce unexpected outcomes, causing delays or stoppage to your project?

By anticipating Unintended Consequences

Unintended Consequences are outcomes that aren't the outcomes expected from your project.

Unintended *Consequences* fall into three categories:

- **A positive**, unexpected benefit, which is usually referred to as serendipity or a windfall.

- **A negative**, unexpected problem like irrigation providing water for agriculture and could also lead to cholera.

- The consequence of **what others might say or do** is referred to as backlash, fallout, or blowback.

Here's an example of a negative *Unintended Consequence*. Can you tell what's wrong with this picture? Hint: Does Starbucks really suck?

Answer: The painters applied the Starbucks advertising on a delivery van with the doors closed. Unfortunately, they failed to consider the unintended consequences of what the van would look like when the side door was open. This is *Murphy's Law* at its best!

By anticipating Second and Third-Order Effects

Be sensitive to how your work affects others.

Second and Third-Order Effects focus on how your work will affect others at different levels in your company.

Different levels mean how your work will affect others in your unit, department, company, and suppliers. *Second and Third-Order Effects* may also identify new resource requirements and cause changes to structures and procedures. For example, if you decide to change a supplier, the effects could be extensive.

- *Second-Order Effects* could require new ordering procedures to be created, which could cause delays.

- *Third-Order Effects* could require others to be retrained on new ordering procedures and software.

To anticipate *Second and Third-Order Effects* keep asking.

Now, what? What's next? What're we forgetting? And what could happen or what might we need to do in 30, 60, or 90 days?

How can you Anticipate Anything?

You're responsible for anticipating the consequences and effects of your work before starting.

But how can you do this when your crystal ball is no less clear than mine?

Method 1: Find others who have dealt with similar problems and ask:

- What problems, consequences, or effects did you have?

- Did everything go as planned? Any do-overs or surprises?

- What outside help did you need, and where did you get it?

- Anything or anyone you didn't have before starting?

- What was the most important and the most difficult task?

- How long did each task take, and what was the cost?

- Anything you'd start, stop, or change next time?

- Was everyone satisfied with the results?

Method 2: Vendors and Suppliers.

Contact vendors and suppliers who have worked with those who have dealt with the same or similar problems and ask the questions from Method 1. Also, which city, county, or state agency must inspect the problem to see if it meets the code?

Method 3: YouTube and Social-Media.

Visit *YouTube* to search for related videos of others who have dealt with the same or similar problems. Then, get on social media and find people who have experienced projects or problems similar to yours. If you find someone, ask the questions from Method 1.

By making changes with CAUTION

Whenever a change is made, there are always consequences and effects. Just because everyone gets the change doesn't mean they understand it. The problem comes later when the consequences and effects start to appear, and everyone is shocked.

Here's a good example:

Bob was the Person-in-Charge of the company's Annual Team Building Session. Two days before the session, Bob's boss (the CFO) called and told him that the venue had been changed to a remote cabin where there was no electricity. Bob called John, the Key Player in-charge of food and beverages, to inform John of the change in venue and the lack of electricity.

The day before the session, Bob followed up with John and was shocked to find that John had not thought through the refrigeration requirements for the food and beverages. Since this was a three-day session, the change of venue not only required ice to be transported to the venue daily but coolers to store it.

John didn't recognize the need for ice, and Bob assumed John had it covered. As a result, the night before the session, both John and Bob spent several hours in the dark, scrambling around looking for coolers and bags of ice to fill them.

All this could have been avoided had John and Bob thought through the consequences and effects created by this last-minute change in venue by testing their assumptions and creating a Plan or Action to deal with it. Not to mention the need for a site recon and a review of the Checklist at Appendix E.

Murphy's Law on Consequences:

"There's never enough time to do it right, but there's always time to do it over."

23
BY BUILDING
CONSENSUS WITH A TEAM

"Unity is strength... when there is teamwork and collaboration, wonderful things can be achieved."
- Mattie Stepanek

Do you know how to achieve agreement from all team members that they can support a proposal? Few people in the workforce today understand the meaning and value of collaborating to build consensus.

The process of building consensus starts with collaboration.

Collaboration is the process of working with others to resolve a problem or achieve a goal.

Building consensus results from collaboration. Most people think that consensus means that everyone must like the proposal, the majority rules, or some other lame criteria - all of which are false.

Here's the truth!

Consensus is the desired end-product of collaboration intended to achieve agreement from all team members that they can support a proposal.

Support means that each member agrees that the proposal will work and commits to doing all they can to ensure its success.

If not, this is their chance to speak up! The process of building consensus gives every member the freedom to voice their agreements or disagreements before consensus is achieved. It's also intended to be inclusive, participatory, and cooperative, seeking opinions and input from all members.

Consensus uses common agreement to resolve mutually exclusive positions. It's not the majority rules, nor a popularity contest. It doesn't care whose proposal is being considered or if any member likes or dislikes the proposal. It only asks each member if they can support the proposal. If not, a valid reason must be provided.

**VALID means that their reason must be either a
better proposal or a fact and not an opinion.**

Why is building consensus important?

To answer this question, I always ask,

What's the Greatest Hunger of the Human Heart?

What does every human being need to be fulfilled at work?

*The Greatest Hunger of the Human Heart
is to be NEEDED.*

To be needed means:

- To be seen means to be included and validated.

- To be heard means to be listened to, understood, and appreciated.

- To be valued means to be recognized for their contributions.

- To be treated with respect and kindness because they matter.

*The greatest hunger of the human heart is to be
seen, heard, valued, and treated with respect
and kindness because they matter.*

If team members aren't allowed to *"speak their piece,"* you're telling them that they're not important and they don't matter. Not good! Do you feel needed where you work? Do those who work with you feel needed? Do you treat everyone with respect and kindness-no matter what?

*Everyone needs to be engaged, involved, and have a say
concerning the things that affect their wellbeing.*

This is why consensus building is so powerful.

When's consensus needed?

Consensus is needed whenever you're trying to resolve a problem, create a plan, or make any change that affects the team.

What are the benefits of building consensus?

- Consensus building improves the proposal by using the wisdom and knowledge of the team.

- It uncovers any Unintended Consequences and Second and Third-Order Effects that could slow or stop the proposal.

- It builds trust and commitment from the team by engaging them and using their input.

Building consensus is far more important than achieving it because, in the end, everyone may not agree to support the proposal, but at least they've been included in the process.

Failure to build consensus will erode teamwork, commitment and cause the failure to consistently produce excellent results. Building consensus sounds easy, but it's not. However, it's worth it because, without their involvement, they'll never be committed! And without their commitment, you'll never be able to consistently produce excellent results!

By building Consensus

Here are two methods of building consensus:

- **Staffing a Proposal.** This means circulating a proposal document through all team members to obtain their concurrence or non-concurrence with comments.

- **Conducting a Team Meeting.** This method works best when the proposal is an important decision that's time-sensitive, involves major funding, and affects the entire team.

If this is the case, here are the most important steps to build consensus.

Step 1. Discuss the proposal.

Gather the team, either at one location or on a phone or video conference, and discuss the proposal.

- **If the proposal is a problem,** how was it discovered, how bad is it, and what're the risks if it continues unresolved? What's causing this problem? Is this the real problem or just a symptom? And how do we know for sure?

- **If the proposal is a goal,** why is it important? What's the intended benefit?

Step 2. Discuss the Solution.

If the solution is obvious, then work with the team to create the *Plan of Action* to implement the solution. If there could be several solutions, conduct a *Brainstorming Session* and select the best solution (Chapter 21).

Step 3. Anticipate the Consequences and Effects.

Once the solution has been identified, discuss the possible *Unintended Consequences* and *Second and Third-Order Effects* (Chapter 11).

Step 4. Eliminate all Unresolved Issues.

Discuss and identify all *Unresolved Issues* (any question, unknown, concern, shortfall, obstacle, or problem) that could slow or stop your progress (Chapter 10).

Step 5. Ask for Consensus.

Now, ask all team members if they can support the proposal. If not, why? Remember,

Support means that each member agrees that the proposal will work and commits to doing all they can to ensure its success.

If all members agree, ask them to create the *Plan of Action* to implement the proposed solution. If any member has a valid reason for non-support, continue to Step 6.

By resolving Reasons for Non-Support

At this point, only valid reasons should be considered. However, real-life doesn't work that way. Members will always have concerns and opinions, and they need to be heard. Here are the most important steps.

Step 6. Deal with their concerns.

If a member has a concern or opinion that's not a fact, this is when things get interesting.

- If their concern is that it's **too costly**, what does he mean? Too costly compared to what? How can the cost be reduced or offset? What's the contingency plan if it does cost more?

- If their concern is that it **will take much longer**, what's he basing this on? What's the downside if it does take longer? What's our Contingency Plan if it does?

- If their concern is that it's **too risky**, what does he mean? Can it be mitigated? Can a contingency plan be created just in case?

Step 7. Convert Reasons to Risks.

Before continuing, exchange the term *"Reason"* for *"Risk."* This will make this process much easier to understand. And for each risk, there are two critical things you must consider, probability and impact.

Step 8. What's the Probability?

How likely is this risk to happen (Chapter 12)? If the probability is *Low*, place the risk, *On-Hold*. This means that it's been noted and set aside temporarily. If the probability is *Medium* to *High*, or you're unsure, continue to the next step.

Step 9. What's the Impact?

What's the Impact or Effect on the proposal when this risk happens (Chapter 12)? If the Impact is *Minor,* place the risk *On-Hold*. If the Impact is *Moderate* to *Significant*, or you're unsure, continue to Step10.

Step 10. Can the Risk be Mitigated?

- If the risk can be mitigated, create a *Contingency Plan* (Chapter 15).

- If the risk can't be mitigated, you still have three options (Chapter 14).

Remember, you don't need a consensus before sending the proposal to your boss for approval. However, you'll need to include all reasons for non-support and let your boss decide. All members don't have to like the solution! They just need to be able to support it.

Here's another method of building consensus without a meeting.

Staffing is the process of circulating a proposal document to all team members to obtain their concurrence or non-concurrence with comments in writing.

This method works best in situations where the proposal is routine and not time-sensitive. The proposal document could be a procedure, plan, question, or idea.

Here are the four most important steps.

Step 1. Provide the proposal document to all members.

Ensure each team member receives a copy of the proposal document. Ask each member for their concurrence or non-concurrence with comments. And don't forget to provide a deadline.

Step 2. Resolve non-concur comments.

When member comments are returned to you, you may need to visit some members privately to better understand their comments and determine if adjusting your proposal could lead to their concurrence. Remember, concurrence means that each member agrees that:

The proposal will work and commits to doing all they can to ensure its success.

If not, a valid reason must be provided, which means their non-concur comments must be a better proposal or a fact and not an opinion.

Step 3. Make changes.

If you need to make changes, you'll need to send the revised proposal to all members again for another review. And for the second review, ensure you highlight any changes made from the first review.

Step 4. Obtain approval.

Note: You don't need the concurrence of all team members before sending your proposal to your boss for approval, but you'll need their reasons for non-concurrence. Remember, building consensus should never be done in a vacuum. You need the feedback to help you see beyond your blind spots.

24
BY CONDUCTING AN
IN-PROGRESS REVIEW

"If I had to live my life again, I'd make the same mistakes, only sooner."
- Tallulah Bankhead.

Do you know how to determine if your project is progressing as planned and if it's ready to move to the next phase?

An In-Progress Review is a synchronization meeting conducted by the Project Manager with all Key Players present to collaborate and coordinate a project.

Each major project will have at least two *IPRs* scheduled between phases of the project.

- **IPR 1** is scheduled at the halfway point of the time remaining (between the Planning and Preparation Phases).

- **IPR 2**, the second or last IPR, is scheduled 5-7 days before the project starts (between the Preparation and the Execution Phases).

IPRs essentially become *Milestones* (A tool used to mark specific points along a project timeline and focus on major progress phases that must be reached before moving forward).

What should be discussed during each IPR?

If this is your project, this is your opportunity to check if everyone involved, especially the *Key Players,* are on-schedule, knows about all changes, and has no *Unresolved Issues* (Chapter 21).

- **Deliverables:** During the IPR, the project's current progress is addressed, and *deliverables* designated in the *POA* are presented. A *deliverable* is something tangible that proves that a Key Player has taken action designated in the *POA* (like a sales receipt, a purchase order, or diagram). If all *deliverables* are present, the project moves to the next phase. If all *deliverables* are not presented, the project is stopped (or delayed) until the boss becomes directly involved for explanations and gives the go-ahead.

- **Unintended Consequences and Second and third-Order Effects (Chapter 22).**

- **Unresolved Issues (Chapter 21).**

25
BY FOLLOWING UP
AND FOLLOWING-THROUGH

"Learning the secrets and skill of great No.2s remains
the surest path to becoming No. 1."
- David Heenan and Warren Bennis.

Do you know how to *Follow up* and *Follow-through* to increase your probability of success and enhance your effectiveness and credibility at work? Many mistakes and failures in business can be traced back to someone who failed to *Follow up or Follow-through*.

By Following up

Follow-up is a subsequent action taken to check on the validity of an initial action.

And there are three situations where *Follow up* is needed.

Situation 1.
When someone fails to respond to your solicitation.

Using a sales example, if a prospect fails to respond to your solicitation or declines to do business with you, you still should *Follow up*. *Follow-up* means continuing to contact them until you receive a positive response. The secret is to continue to add value to the person you're trying to contact.

Situation 2.
When you're trying to contact someone to resolve a problem.

Here are the most important steps if you're trying to resolve a problem (like poor customer service, a faulty product, or a delayed order).

Step 1. Call to resolve the problem.

Record the date you called, whom you spoke with, and the response you received.

Step 2. Leave a detailed voicemail message.

If you get their voicemail, always leave a message giving the date, your name, company, phone number, a detailed description of the problem with its reference number, and a request for a return call.

Step 3. Document your actions.

Always document your *follow-up* action. This way, when your boss asks, you can show him your *"Action Log."*

Step 4. Show up in person.

After you've called three times with no response, show up in person and get your problem resolved.

Step 5. Add it to your Unresolved Issues List.

Until resolved, keep this issue on your *Unresolved Issues List* and ensure your boss has a current copy (Chapter 21).

Situation 3.
After delegating an assignment or making a reservation or appointment.

Follow-up also means contacting someone a few days before the due date of your assignment, reservation, or appointment to confirm it's still valid.

Delegating an assignment isn't abdication because the asker is still responsible and accountable for the end-result.

5% of delegating is asking someone to perform a task. The other 95% is about following up to ensure it gets done.

A good 30% of the time, my reservations or appointments got lost. I assumed that all was good-to-go, and I was sadly mistaken.

Here's a great story of how it should be done

On June 1st, Joe was asked by his boss to set up a luncheon for 30 senior executives at the best steak house in town for June 15th.

This was two weeks before the luncheon when Joe made the initial reservation. He recorded the date, time, and the name of the person he spoke with on his Assignment Tracking Form (Appendix F).

On June 12th, a few days before the luncheon, as Joe was reviewing his Assignment Tracking Form, he decided to follow up, and here's how it went. Hi, this is Joe Sanchez from Trident Resources. I'm calling to follow up on the reservation for our company's luncheon for Thursday, June 15th, at 11:30 AM? Is everything still on track?

The scheduler said, "Joe, I don't have a reservation for your company. When did you make it, and whom did you speak with? After looking at his Assignment Tracking Form, Joe said, "I called two weeks ago, on June 1st, and I spoke to Carol Brown."

After a long pause, the scheduler continued, "Carol was let go two weeks ago. That may explain the problem. Then, after another long pause, she said, "Joe, you're lucky. You called just in time. If you had waited another day, you'd be out of luck." After Joe's heart rate returned to normal, he was glad he documented all his phone calls and followed up when he did. If not, he would have had 30 senior executives standing around looking for a place to eat. Not good.

By Following-through

This is what your boss means when he says, *"Get back to me, let me know, or keep me in the loop."*

Follow-through is the process of returning to the asker, either face-to-face or on the phone, and reporting the status of their request.

There are two situations where *Follow-through* is needed.

Situation 1.
When your boss or customer asks you to do something.

When this happens, make sure you have a clear understanding of what the boss or customer wants to be done (the task) and when he needs it completed (the deadline). If you have any questions, ask! If you can't deliver, speak up! After completing the task, *Return and Report*, either face-to-face or on the phone.

Return and Report mean contacting the asker, either face-to-face or on the phone, to update the status of their request. If you can't complete the task as requested, return, either face-to-face or on the phone, and report the problem. Also, recommend what should be done to resolve the problem.

Returning and Reporting is the most important part of Following-through.

Situation 2.
When you ask a Direct Report to do something.

When you ask a Direct Report to do something, ensure you tell him WHAT you want to be done (the task) and WHEN you need it completed (the deadline).

Also, ask him to *Follow-through*. You may have to explain what you mean. Explain that you want him to *Return and Report*, either face-to-face or on the phone when the task is completed. If he can't complete the task, ask him to return, either face-to-face or on the phone, and report the problem and recommend what needs to be done to resolve it.

The most effective people I know, those at the *top of their game*, do something special.

They over-communicate!

They Follow-through even if they have nothing new.

This way, I know I wasn't forgotten!

When you *Follow-through*, you'll stand out above the rest.

Note: When you tell someone that *"I'm-on-it,"* you've just told them that you'll *Follow-through*.

26
BY MANAGING
RISK

There is only one big risk you should avoid at all costs,
and that is the risk of doing nothing."
- Denis Waitley

Do you know how to manage the risk associated with your work?

Simply Stated, RISK is Uncertainty!

Managing anything requires the ability to anticipate and mitigate risk. You can't control everything that happens to you, but you can control your degree of preparation and how you respond.

Here are the most important things to consider when assessing risk.

1. Reduce the Risk of Failure.

By planning for risk to occur, you're decreasing your probability of failure, which increases your probability of success. Much of this is done every day in your company. It's called risk reduction, like having fire, theft, and liability insurance.

2. Understand that control is an illusion.

This simple prayer, which I learned during my recovery from alcoholism, helped me finally answer this life-altering question:

What are the only things in life I can

control and therefore change?

THE SERENITY PRAYER

"God, grant me the <u>Serenity</u> to

<u>Accept</u> the things I cannot change,

<u>Courage</u> to change the things I can,

and the <u>Wisdom</u> to know the difference

- Reinhold Niebuhr

And these answers changed my life forever.

In this life,
You cannot control or change other people,
places, things, situations, or circumstances.

The only things you can control and therefore
change are your thoughts, words, and deeds.

And all those years, I thought I could control and change other people. What a waster of time and energy. This may come as a shocking epiphany for many of you because you've probably made the same mistake.

Yes, you can influence them, but you can't
control or change them. You can only control
and therefore change yourself.

This concept is crucial because until you learn to truly control what you can control (your thoughts, words, and deeds), you'll never influence anyone to help you consistently produce excellent results.

3. Identify your Risk Goals.

When it comes to managing risk, you should always have two goals.

- Make the **Risk** LESS likely to happen, like putting training wheels on your child's bicycle.

- Make the **Impact** LESS severe when, and NOT if it happens, like requiring your child to wear a safety helmet.

4. Plan for both Anticipated and Unanticipated Risk.

In life, there are always two categories of risk:

- **Anticipated Risks** are those risks that include all the things that could *reasonably-go-wrong*, including anything that could slow or stop your project or cause injury, illness, accident, death, security violations, property damage, or financial loss.

- **Unanticipated Risks** are those Risks that you could not possibly have predicted (Chapter 30).

5. Conduct a Risk Assessment.

With the help of your team, conduct a *Risk Assessment*.

Anticipated Risk comes in two forms:

- **Bad Internal Situations** are things that don't require a call to 911, like equipment breakdowns, people being late, cell phone batteries going dead, and other mistakes, defects, or errors.

- **Bad External Situations** are things that will require a call to 911, like fire, injuries, accidents, property damage, violence, or theft.

6. Assess the Impact and Probability.

For each Bad Situation, assess these two critical things:

- **Impact** means how this Bad Situation will affect your project and is rated as *Significant, Moderate, or Minor*. Based on your assessment, when, and not if, this Bad Situation happens, how serious will it affect your project?

- **Probability** means how likely is this Bad Situation to happen and is rated as *High, Medium, or Low*. Based on your assessment, how likely is this Bad Situation to occur?

7. Assess your Risk Options.

Option 1. AVOID the Risk.

In some cases, you may want to avoid the risk altogether. This could mean not getting involved or just deleting a high-risk activity. This is a good option when taking the risk involves no advantage or when the cost of mitigating isn't worth the risk.

However, when you avoid a potential risk entirely, you may miss an opportunity. So, do your *What if Analysis* to explore your options before deciding. To learn more, search *YouTube* for *"What if analysis on Excel."*

Option 2. SHARE the Risk!

You could decide to share the risk and the potential gain with others. For example, you share risks when you ensure your project site or partner with another company.

Option 3. ACCEPT the Risk.

This option is usually best under these conditions:

- When there's nothing you can do to prevent the risk.

- When the potential loss is less than the cost of insuring against the risk.

- When the potential gain is worth accepting the risk.

For example, you might accept the risk of a project launching late if the potential sales will still cover your costs.

8. Beware of Scope Creep.

Scope means the size of the project and its requirements, complexity, and goals. Scope creep occurs when others want to make changes to your project. So, negotiate these changes to gain either more time or more money, or both.

9. Create Contingency Plans.

The purpose of any *Contingency Plan* (Chapter 30) is to diminish the severity of a bad situation when it occurs. *Contingency Plans* need to be *Staffed* (Chapter 23) through all Key Players and approved by the boss.

10. Use Preventive Actions.

Mistakes are not a problem if they're caught before they get in front of your boss or the customer.

What *Assessment Systems* (Chapter 6) do you have to catch mistakes? Effective people anticipate and mitigate their risk by adding *Preventive Actions* to their *Project's Timetable* (Chapter 5).

27
BY CONDUCTING A
RISK ASSESSMENT

"Take risks: if you win, you will be happy;
if you lose, you will be wise."
- Unknown

Effective people know that conducting a good *Risk Assessment* is critical to their probability of success. You can't control everything that happens to you, but you can control your degree of preparation and how you respond. With the help of your team, conduct a good *Risk Assessment* by *Brainstorming* (Chapter 29) anything related to your work that could *reasonably-go-wrong*.

Here are the most important steps to conduct a good *Risk Assessment*.

Step 1. Anticipate the Physical Risks.

Have you inspected the site for anything that could cause an injury, accident, illness, or death? How about safety, sanitation, and access for those with disabilities - any risk there?

Step 2. Anticipate the Security Risks.

- For **cybersecurity,** what could cause a data breach, personal info or intellectual property loss, or a disruption of services?

- For **physical security**, what could permit unauthorized access leading to theft or property damage?

Step 3. Anticipate the Financial Risk.

- What could cause financial loss through fraud, waste, or abuse?

- What insurance is needed, and is it current?

Step 4. Anticipate the Operational Risks.

- What's the *Impact* when these risks occur (Chapter 26)?

- What's the *Probability* that these risks will happen (Chapter 26)?

- How can these risks be mitigated (Chapter 28)?

- What's your *Contingency Plan* for when they do (Chapter 30)?

- Do your team members know how to take *Immediate Action* (Appendix B)?

- What assumptions are needed to move the work forward (Appendix D)?

- What *Preventive Actions* did you add to your *Plan of Action (POA) Timetable* (Chapter 4-5).

- Have you *Staffed* your POA (Chapter 23) with the team, and what was the result?

- What are you forgetting to do (Appendices E)?

Step 5. Eliminate Unresolved Issues.

What are all the questions, unknowns, concerns, shortfalls, obstacles, or problems that could slow or stop our progress (Chapter 21)?

Step 6. Anticipate and Mitigate Unintended Consequences.

Unintended Consequences are the outcomes that aren't expected by your actions (Chapter 22).

Step 7. Anticipate Second and Third-Order Effects.

Second and Third-Order Effects focus on how your recommendations or decisions affect others at different levels in your organization (Chapter 22).

Step 8. Anticipate the Risk of Bad Situations.

- **Bad Internal Situations** are situations that *don't require a call to 911*, like equipment breakdowns, people being late, cell phone batteries going dead, mistakes, defects, or errors.

- **Bad External Situations** are situations that *require a call to 911,* like fire, injuries, accidents, property damage, violence, or theft (Chapter 28).

If you fail to conduct a good *Risk Assessment* before your next project, do so at your peril.

You've been WARNED!

28
BY MITIGATING THE RISK
TO BAD SITUATIONS

"If you are not living on the edge, you are taking up too much room."
- Jayne Howard

Do you know how to mitigate the risks associated with your work? To manage anything, you need to know how to mitigate your risk. In business, there are two different types of risk: Internal and External.

By mitigating the Risk to Bad Internal Situations

This includes equipment breakdowns, people being late, cell phone batteries going dead, and other mistakes, defects, or errors.

Bad Internal Situations are situations that don't require a call to 911.

Once you've determined everything that could *reasonably-go-wrong*, you're ready to mitigate the risks. Here are the most important steps.

Step 1. Brainstorm.

Conduct a *Brainstorming Session* to determine what actions are needed to respond to each bad situation (Chapter 29).

Step 2. Create Contingency Plans.

Now that you've determined what actions are needed for each Bad Internal Situation, it's time to create a *CONPLAN* for each (Chapter 30).

Step 3. Rehearse each CONPLAN.

Rehearse each *CONPLAN* a few days before your project to identify any errors, omissions, or misunderstandings. Don't just ask people if they're ready. Ask them to show you that they're ready (Chapter 31).

Step 4. Eliminate All Unresolved Issues.

Continue to eliminate all *Unresolved Issues* by facilitating collaborative *problem-solving to build consensus (Chapter 21).

*To learn more about *Problem-Solving*, available at **Amazon.com,** see page 5.

By mitigating the Risk to Bad External Situations

The truth is that even though local first responders have more resources and training than you, you can still make the risk less likely to happen and make the impact less severe when it occurs.

Bad External Situations are those that require a call to 911.

Here are the most important steps to mitigate the risk of Bad External Situations.

Step 1. Assess the Risk of Fire.

Since most fires start as small fires, do you have more fire extinguishers on-site than you need? Do people know where they're located and how to use them? Have they been tested and inspected? Are there sufficient smoke detectors present and serviceable? Are there any local restrictions on burning, building fires, or fire warnings?

Step 2. Assess the Risk of Medical Issues.

Do you have first aid kits on-site, with staff trained on how to administer first aid? When were these kits last inspected and replenished? Can ambulances be located closer to your venue? Do you have staff trained to administer CPR? Do defibrillators be centrally located with staff trained in how to use them?

What about those who have food allergies and those allergic to bee stings? And how about mosquitos, the elderly, and the disabled? Are there any unsafe conditions that could lead to an injury or accident? Are there any unsanitary conditions that could lead to illness?

Step 3. Assess the Risk of Crime.

Whenever assessing the risk of crime, always consider:

- **Access control** means entry denial, metal detectors, gates, locks, keys, fences, barriers, checkpoints, firewalls, passwords, and badges.

- **Deterrence** means cameras, guards, dogs, signs, security lighting, punishment for violators, and barbed wire.

- **Early warning** means alarms, security systems, loudspeakers, intercom, flashing lights, police alerts, lockdowns, and sirens.

29

BY CONDUCTING A
BRAINSTORMING SESSION

"To win without risk is to triumph without glory."
- Pierre Corneille

How many times have you just assumed that you knew the BEST solution to a problem, only to find out later that you were wrong? Effective people know the value of *Brainstorming* when resolving problems and achieving goals.

Brainstorming is a group process of producing the most potential options to resolve a problem or achieve a goal.

Here are the most important steps.

Step 1. Pick your team.

Keep your group small (seven or less). If more than seven members, break them into smaller groups and compare the results.

Step 2. Use Mindstorming (Optional!).

The day before, give each team member a sealed envelope with instructions not to open it until they get home that night. Inside the envelope are instructions to conduct a *Mindstorming Exercise* by writing down many potential options for a problem. Also, ask them not to share their options before the meeting the next day.

Step 3. Prepare needed materials.

You'll need a blackboard, whiteboard, or some large sheets of paper on a vertical easel, wide-tipped markers to record all options for all to see.

Step 4. Decide how you'll participate.

Some members may not feel comfortable if you conduct the session. If you ever feel that your presence could diminish the team's effectiveness, find something else to do.

Step 5. Assign other duties.

If needed, select someone else to facilitate the *Brainstorming Session* and assign another member to act as the *Scribe* to record each option.

Step 6. Conduct the meeting.

A good *Brainstorming Session* should consist of these three phases.

Phase I. Capture All Options:

Limit this phase to 10-15 minutes or just enough time for each member to present their options. In this phase, you're looking for volume only. Judgment or criticism is reserved for the next phase.

Phase II. Discuss all Options:

After capturing everyone's options, this phase is where discussion is encouraged and options are consolidated.

Phase III. Validate each Option by using the *"Common-Sense Test:"*

This phase is designed to assess the validity of each option by using the ***Common-Sense Test.*** This test asks five questions about each option to qualify it as a valid option. If any option receives a *"No"* or *"we're not sure"* answer, it's eliminated.

    1. Is it Suitable? Does the option solve the problem, and is it legal and ethical?

    2. Is it Feasible? Does it fit within available or easily acquirable resources?

    3. Is it Acceptable? Is it worth the cost and the risk?

    4. Is it Distinguishable? Does it differ significantly from other options?

    5. Is it Complete? Does it solve the problem from start to finish?

Step 7. Select the Best.

In the end, you should have a list of valid options that require further research to help you select the best option. *Brainstorming* helps build commitment. Since you've included the team in the selection process, they'll be more committed when the time comes to implement the best option.

Involvement builds commitment, and commitment is critical to the consistent production of excellent results.

30

BY CREATING
CONTINGENCY PLANS

"If you don't risk anything you risk even more."
- Erica Jong

Do you know how to create a plan to respond to anticipated bad situations?

By creating a Contingency Plan

A Contingency Plan (or CONPLAN) is a Plan of Action that assumes that an anticipated bad situation has occurred.

Have you ever been involved with a project when things went wrong? What did you do? Was there a *Contingency Plan,* and was it rehearsed? A *CONPLAN* is only executed when something bad happens. Being prepared is the key! What's your plan? Remember,

Many bad situations never become a problem
because someone knew what to do and had
the resources to respond.

Here are the most important steps.

Step 1. Collaborate.

Once you've identified all the bad things that could *reasonably-go-wrong,* collaborate with your team to determine what actions should be taken in response.

Step 2. Assess the Impact.

Impact means how this Bad Situation will affect your project and is rated as *Significant, Moderate, or Minor.* Based on your assessment, when, and not if, this Bad Situation happens, how serious will it affect your project?

Step 3. Assess the Probability.

Probability means how likely is this Bad Situation to happen and is rated as *High, Medium, or Low*. Based on your assessment, how likely is this Bad Situation to occur? If you have a bad situation with a Significant Impact and a High Probability of occurring, you'll need lots of help.

Step 4. Create a CONPLAN.

Once you've identified the actions that should be taken, create a CONPLAN to deal with each Bad Situation. Each CONPLAN uses the same format as a *Plan of Action* but begins with an assumption.

This assumption is the Bad Situation that you and your team have already anticipated. Your CONPLAN tells the reader exactly what to do when the assumption becomes true. It also lists what's needed, where it's stored, and how to use it.

Let's assume that you were assigned as the Project Manager for your company's *Team Building Session* in Buffalo, NY, in January. You and your team have already anticipated three Bad Internal Situations that could *reasonably-go-wrong* with your project.

- **For guests arriving late,** you assessed the Impact to be *Significant* because the Team Building Session won't be effective without all guests. However, you assessed your probability to be *Medium* because of the weather in Buffalo this time of year. So, for guests arriving late, you intend to use CONPLAN A.

- **For transporting guests to the resort,** you assessed the Impact to be *Moderate* because of the weather, the fact that the resort is 27 miles away, and that delays will disrupt the success of the team building session. And you assessed the probability to be *Medium* because you know that the weather in Buffalo this time of year is always a challenge. So, for Transporting guests to the resort, you intend to use CONPLAN B.

- **For lost baggage,** you assessed the Impact to be *Minor* because your activity can still go on regardless. However, you assessed the Probability to be *High* because the airlines in the winter have a history of losing luggage. So, for lost baggage, you intend to use CONPLAN C.

Step 5. Create your Risk Matrix.

Here's an example of a *Risk Matrix*.

Risk Matrix for Team Building Session			
BAD SITUATION	**IMPACT**	**PROBABILITY**	**CONPLAN**
Guests Arriving Late	Significant (8-10)	Medium (4-7)	A
Transport to Resort	Moderate (4-7)	Medium (4-7)	B
Lost Baggage	Minor (1-3)	High (8-10)	C

Notice that this simple table shows all Bad Internal Situations, their Impact, Probability, and which CONPLAN to use.

Note: The risk numbers 1 through 10 above are used to help create your *Risk Threshold*.

Step 6. Assess your Risk Threshold.

Here's an example of a *Risk Threshold Table*.

Risk Threshold = Impact X Probability.		
Risk Rating	**Risk Range**	**Remarks**
CRITICAL	50 or higher	The acceptable risk threshold for safety and health should always be lower than your financial or operational risks.
MEDIUM	16 to 49	
LOW	15 or Lower	

Notice that this table shows that a *risk threshold*, rated from critical to medium to low, is the sum of the impact times the probability. Knowing your risk threshold is important because your acceptable safety and health risk threshold should always be lower than your financial or operational risks. Ideally, you should be doing all you can to reduce your risk. And if you can't, you'll need a good CONPLAN ready to respond, and it needs to be rehearsed.

Step 7. Staff your CONPLANs.

Staff your CONPLANs through all Key Players for their concurrence or non-concurrence with comments (Chapter 23).

Step 8. Obtain Approval.

Present your CONPLANs to your boss for approval with all the comments from your Key Players attached.

Step 9. Distribute your CONPLANs.

Once approved, ensure that all Key Players have a copy of all CONPLANs well before the project starts.

Step 10. Rehearse your CONPLANs.

A few days before your project starts, rehearse your CONPLANs with all Key Players (Chapter 31).

By creating an Unanticipated Situation Plan

Do you know how to create a plan to respond to unanticipated bad situations?

An Unanticipated Situation Plan is a Contingency Plan that assumes that an unanticipated bad situation will occur.

When unanticipated bad situations occur, what do you do? Is that even possible? Preparing for *Unanticipated Bad Situations* requires a different level of thinking and preparation. Regardless of how well you plan, you'll always encounter bad situations that you did not, nor could not have anticipated. So, what do you do?

As a Project Manager, what will you do when an *Unanticipated Bad Situation* occurs on your watch? Your boss is counting on you to do everything you can to save, salvage, or secure your project.

You already know that many Bad Situations never become problems because someone responded to them swiftly and decisively. They had *Assessment Systems* (Chapter 6) and people in place to respond to these situations when they occurred. They saved the day!

You can't control everything that happens to you.
But you can control your degree of preparation
and how you respond.

But how did they do it? They did it by creating an *Unanticipated Situation Plan,* a type of *Contingency Plan* that focuses on *Unanticipated Risk.*

Here are three special techniques that will help you prepare for and respond to *Unanticipated Bad Situations.*

1. Create a Quick Response Team (or QRT).

A *QRT* is a team specifically trained and equipped (with vehicle, keys, access codes, cash, and credit cards) on *Stand-by* (they have no other duties and are ready to respond, 24/7). Provide a sketch map to all *QRT* members that shows all locations to use as reference points.

2. Use a Priority Response System.

The system is a cellphone protocol that requires that all Key Players:

- Respond to their cell phone before the <u>second</u> ring.
- Have extra batteries and car chargers easily available.
- Carry their cell phone on their person 24/7.
- Never let incoming calls from you go to voicemail.
- Have all contact numbers of all Key Players on their phones.
- Limit their outgoing calls to ensure they're able to respond.

This system is only effective if everyone plays by these rules. This is why it should be rehearsed. When you call, you need the Key Player to answer before the <u>second</u> ring - no excuses.

3. Create a Pre-Stocking Site.

This site is stocked with any materials, equipment, and supplies that could cause a delay or stoppage of your project.

- Do you have backup bulbs, projectors, and extension cords?
- Do you have backup batteries and AC and DC chargers?
- Where will these items be located?
- Does your boss and all Key Players know this location?

Have one trusted Key Player responsible for this site, ready to deliver what, when, and where it's needed. Also, this site could be mobile, like a van or truck pre-positioned at or near the site, as needed.

Always be prepared to take *Immediate Action* (Appendix B).

By creating a Mitigation Plan

No one likes being on a project when things are going badly. So, how can you get the project back *on track*?

A Mitigation Plan is a POA designed to get a project back on track by eliminating, consolidating, or rescheduling certain tasks to finish close to the originally planned date.

Here are the most important questions to ask if you ever have a project in trouble:

- Are there any tasks that can be eliminated, combined, **or** compressed?
- Is there **Slack Time* that can be used?
- Can anything be done simultaneously (or done *off-line*)?
- Do you need more people? Can overtime help?
- Should you go to a second shift or run 24-hours?
- Can working on the weekend and holidays help?
- Can the scope (size, requirements, complexity, goals) be reduced?
- Can the end time be moved to allow a successful completion?

*Slack time: The amount of time in a schedule that a task can be delayed without causing a delay to other tasks or the project's completion date.

Getting behind schedule isn't fun. How does any project get thirty days behind? Answer: one day at a time, repeated thirty times. So, what's the message here? Don't get behind in the first place!

For those of you who think you'll never have to create a *Mitigation Plan* in your lifetime, think again. If you have a plan for getting your college education, MBA, or a Ph.D., what happens if you must take a year off? It's called a *Mitigation Plan* to help you pick up the pieces and move forward.

31
BY CONDUCTING A
REHEARSAL

"Take calculated risks. That is quite different from being rash."
- George S. Patton

Do you know how to identify and correct any *Pre-Problems* that could slow or stop your progress?

By Rehearsing

A Rehearsal is the process of reviewing (looking at) the results of others before they get in front of your boss to ensure all Pre-Problems (mistakes, defects, shortfalls, omissions, or errors) have been resolved.

The type of rehearsal I'm referring to here is to examine everything concerning your project BEFORE your boss sees it. How hard is that?

Why do you think weddings have rehearsals?

Do you have the ring, know where to stand, know what to say, and know the sequence of what's going to happen next? And why does it matter? Who wants it to be perfect? Enough said. What do you need to see, test, or practice a few days before your project starts?

Get a Clue! Even criminals have rehearsals because they know the consequences if they don't.

Rehearsals include things like previews, layouts, practice, a sand-table, or white-board walk-throughs. They also include demonstrations, role-playing, document reviews, and testing. And when your rehearsal uncovers a flaw, have it fixed and have another rehearsal.

Caution! Never ask people, *"are you ready?"* Instead, say, *"Show me that you're ready. I want to see it!"* What's stopping you?

Look, I can't tell you how many times I've been burned by people who've said to me that they were ready when they weren't. So, do yourself a favor. If this is your project, your job is to check. That means looking at everything before it gets in front of your boss.

By Practicing

As a child, I was told that *"Practice makes perfect."* As an adult, I learned that this was false. It should be,

Perfect practice makes perfect.

If you're practicing the wrong way, your results will suffer. That's why you always need a coach, someone who can show you how it should be done correctly to achieve the best result.

My favorite practice quote comes from **Coach Paul *"Bear"* Bryant**.

> **"It's not the will to win that matters – everyone has that. It's the will to prepare (or practice) to win that matters."**

It's no wonder Coach Bryant amassed six national championships and thirteen conference championships as the head coach of the University of Alabama's football team.

Growing up, I also learned that to be the best, I needed to *"Practice until I got it right."* However, much later in life, I found that to master anything, I needed to

Practice until I couldn't get it wrong.

The best example of this comes from **Mary Lou Retton,** who won the gold medal in the 1984 Olympics in LA. She scored a perfect 10 in the vault competition.

After that vault, she asked the judges if she could do it again to show it wasn't just a lucky vault. Her score was another perfect 10. More impressive was that she was a sophomore in high school, had recently had leg surgery, and won two silver medals and two bronze medals.

Her performance was historic because she was the first-ever American woman to win the all-around gold medal at the Olympics, making her the most popular athlete in the US.

32
BY CONDUCTING AN
AFTER-ACTION REVIEW

"We don't have a crisis of leadership in Washington.
We have a crisis of followership."
- Jonathan Rauch

How can you enhance your performance and the performance of your team? One way is to use *After-Action Reviews.*

An After-Action Review (AAR) is a professional discussion conducted after an activity, with all members present, seeking ways to consistently improve the way things are done.

AARs should be conducted both during (at the end of each day) and the day after an activity (project, objective, or goal) by measuring the difference between what was supposed to happen (the Plan) vs. what did happen (Behavior and Results).

AARs observe, measure, record, and assess an activity or process from start to finish to examine the results and the behavior of those involved.

The purpose of an AAR is to:

- Capture and share intuition by asking HOW and WHY questions.

- Attempt to discover WHY things happen and how to get better.

- Help members understand HOW and WHY decisions are made.

- Encourage members to become *self-correcting* and more aware of how their behavior affects others (Appendix G).

- Capture *Lessons Learned* to integrate into future operations.

Here are the four most important steps to conducting an AAR:

Step 1. The Objective.

Before the activity (project, objective, or goal): What are we trying to achieve? What performance standards and results are desired? Who and what will be observed, and how will it be measured?

Step 2. The Results and Behavior.

During the activity: What happened? What was observed and measured? What are the facts?

Step 3. The Assessment.

After the activity: Did things go as expected? Were there any surprises? If the result wasn't what we expected, what should be started, stopped, or changed to achieve a better result? WHY and HOW did we do what we did?

Step 4. The Lessons Learned.

What did we learn that can help us do better next time?

By using Informal After-Action Reviews

Let's assume that you're the Project Manager for a four-day Trade Show and you have three team members.

The week before the show, you and your boss sat down to discuss the plan and its objective. Why are we attending this show? What's the ideal outcome you'd like to see? How will this outcome be measured? After finishing with your boss, you met with your team and briefed them on the plan.

Fast forward to the end of the first day of the show. You assembled your team and asked, what did we learn today that can make us better tomorrow? One team member said it would have been nice to have some bottled water in our booth. A second member said, we also need a lunch schedule, so everyone has a chance to eat. Also, we're running low on our advertising brochures. You then asked one team member to provide bottled water in the booth every day. Then you asked another member to set up a lunch schedule for each day. And finally, you called your boss and asked him to overnight a bunch of advertising brochures. You also conducted an informal review at the end of each day with the goal of continuous improvement.

The day after the trade show, you gathered your team together and asked if we accomplished our goal? Did everything go as planned? Were there any surprises? What did we learn that could make the next Trade Show better? You then added all comments to your After-Action Report so next year's Trade Show can be even better. How hard was that?

33
BY ASSESSING PERFORMANCE

"Followership, like leadership, is a role and not a destination."
- Michael McKinney

How will your boss assess your performance? Your performance at work includes your results, behavior, and potential.

Effective people don't just set the bar; they are the bar.

Are they getting better or worse? How do you know for sure?

What's the best way to assess performance?

The best way to assess performance is by using solid, objective measurements. Actual performance measurement is a more effective way to evaluate results because the measurement is relevant to the situation or process. Some of the best ways to assess performance are by using *Metrics, Objectives and Key Results (OKRs)*, *Key Performance Indicators (KPIs), and Bands of Excellence (BOEs).*

By using Metrics

Metrics are quantifiable and allow you to set the desired result compared to the actual result, but there's a downside.

A metric is something used to measure and track the results of members, teams, or systems to assess its performance.

Here's a good story:

Bob was assigned to improve the number of "problem fixes per day" called into the Helpdesk in his company. He spent a few hours in the Helpdesk Call Center to observe. To his amazement, he found that each Helpdesk Operator was assessed daily using 17 different metrics. One metric was how much "time the operator spent on the phone."

The operators were told to keep each call to less than two minutes, which was counterproductive in solving the caller's problems. After a few hours, Bob determined that working under these conditions (metrics) was not a good place to work.

His intuition told him that the metrics were too restrictive. He directed that all metrics be stopped except for one; the number of "problems fixed per day."

Result? The number of *"problems fixed per day"* shot up off the charts. Problem solved! So, be careful with all your metrics. Sometimes less is more. Focus on the most important metrics – the ones that make sense.

Here are some typical metrics.

- **Cash Flow:** Cash flow is the money coming in and out of your business on any given day, which is what you use to cover your business expenses, such as payroll, rent, and inventory.

- **Customer: Customer Acquisition Cost (CAC).** Divide your total acquisition costs by the number of new customers over the same time frame you're examining.

- **Employee: Employee Turnover Rate (ETR).** To determine your ETR, take the number of employees who have departed the company and divide it by the average number of employees. If you have a high ETR, spend some time examining your workplace culture, employment packages, and work environment.

By using Objectives and Key Results (OKRs)

An OKR (or Objectives and Key Results) is a framework for defining and tracking objectives and their outcomes.

OKR is generally attributed to **Andy Grove**, CEO of Intel, who introduced the approach to Intel during his tenure there and documented this in his 1983 book *High Output Management*. OKRs comprise an **O**bjective, a clearly defined goal, and one or more **K**ey **R**esults (specific measures used to track the achievement of that objective).

OKRs:

- It may be shared across the company to provide teams with visibility of goals to align and focus effort.

- Are typically set at the company, team, and personal levels, although there is criticism on this causing too much of a waterfall approach, which OKRs in many ways are just the opposite.

- Overlap with other performance management frameworks - complexity sitting somewhere between KPI and the balanced scorecard.

The idea took hold, and OKRs quickly became central to Google's culture as a "management methodology" that helps ensure that the company focuses effort on the same important issues throughout the company."

Since becoming popular at Google, OKR has favored several similar tech start-ups, including LinkedIn, Twitter, and Uber. For more on OKRs, review the book or audiobook, *Measure What Matters* by **John Doerr**.

By using Key Performance Indicators (KPI)

KPIs provide a company with a focus for strategic and operational improvement and compare achievements to similar companies.

A Key Performance Indicator (KPI) is a performance measure that demonstrates how effectively a company is at achieving its key objectives.

To be effective, a *KPI* must be well-defined and quantifiable, communicated throughout your company, crucial to achieving the goal, and applicable to the business.

What's the difference between a Metric and a KPI?

- *KPIs* support business goals and objectives.

- *Metrics* support *KPIs* and focus on the overall tactical business goals and objectives.

Meaningful performance measures start with measurable goals. This means that your goal needs to be clear enough that you can imagine how you'll recognize it when it becomes real. So, you might first want to check if your current goals are measurable. Members won't *buy-in* to something they don't understand, weren't involved with, and see no relevance.

The key to deriving *KPIs* from objectives is to work backward and reverse engineer the *metrics* you want to create. This process is called goal, question, metric. Your objectives are your goals for your business or project.

By using Bands of Excellence (BOE)

Since *Public-Sector Organizations,* like teachers or government workers, don't focus on profit generation, what matters most to their survival is providing a service that serves the greater good (like schools and government agencies). But how do they do that? They use a metric called a *Band of Excellence (or BOE)* to measure and assess their level of services.

Those who work in the Public-Sector must maintain their *Band of Excellence (BOE)* set by their organization. Think of *BOEs* as the desired Standard of Performance for members, units, and systems.

A Band of Excellence is a set of performance limits ranging from the Minimum (or Standard)performance limit to the Maximum performance limit.

The difference between the minimum and the maximum is called the *Band of Excellence.* If your performance stays within the *Band of Excellence,* you remain employable.

Here's a simple example.

The biggest government agency on the planet is the US Department of Defense. In 1992, as a former US Army Officer, here's the BOE used to measure physical fitness by taking the Annual Physical Fitness Test.

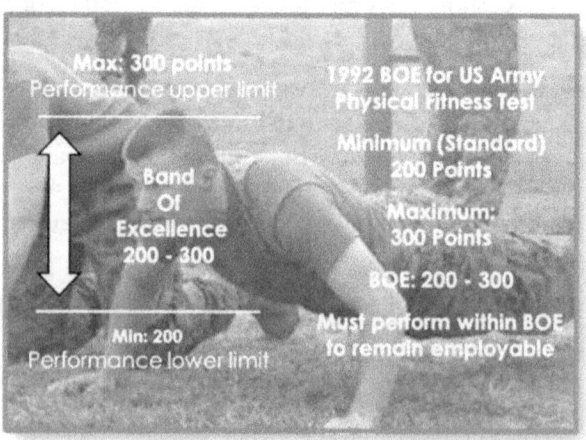

The BOE Minimum (or Standard) was 200 points overall. The BOE Maximum was 300 points overall. The BOE was 200 - 300 for the test overall to remain promotable.

If a Soldier failed to achieve 200 points overall, he was retrained and retested. If he failed a second time, he was considered un-promotable and administratively processed for release from the military.

By Tracking Trends

Have you ever tried to measure how you and your unit were doing? If not, you will. In every viable business, key metrics help determine the answer to one simple question: Are we getting better *Over-Time*?

Over-time means as compared to a past time (last month or year).

And ask the same question about yourself, *are you getting better over time?* And your business unit, *is my business unit getting better over time?* But how can you tell?

Here's a good example:

Think of KPIs as your Doctor does when you go for a physical.

- ***Step 1:*** *What gets measured? They measure the most important aspects of optimum health, like weight, height, blood pressure, pulse, temperature, and cholesterol.*

- ***Step 2:*** *If this is your first physical, how do your numbers compare to a healthy person your age (what's the norm, standard, or benchmark)? Any corrective action needed?*

- ***Step 3:*** *If this isn't your first physical, how do your numbers compare to your last physical? Are you (your physical system) getting better over time? Any corrective action needed?*

Use this same process with all your Key Performance Indicators. What are the things you can measure that tell you about the health of your unit?

Are you getting better over time?

If not, why? What can be done (corrective action) to reverse the numbers? What number is acceptable to you? What are your standards? If this number rises above or falls below a certain level, what *corrective action* must be taken? Trends.

One way to visually track your *KPIs* is to measure and compare your numbers *over-time*, the trend. What does the trend look like? Is it trending in the right direction? By doing so, you'll be able to see if the trend is getting better or worse.

Here's an example of Tracking Trends.

Accounts Receivable, 90-Days Past Due (As of June 21, 20XX)			
This month	**Last month**	**2-Months ago**	**1-Year Ago**
$15,335	$12,457	$10,237	$25,936

Notice that this table is tracking a *Key Performance Indicator* that measures *Accounts Receivable over a 90-day period*. The current status ("This Month") is greater than last month and the month before. In other words, your *90-Day Past Due* numbers are increasing or getting worse.

Tip: Check the usage rate or consumption rate metrics for your unit over-time and see what you learn.

34
BY ASSESSING
RESULTS

"Incremental progress leads to long-lasting results."
- Frank Sonnenberg

How will your boss assess your results? Your results deal with what you've achieved and include your actual job outputs, countable products, measurable outcomes, and accomplishments. They're normally measured objectively (with numbers and metrics), but not always. Your results don't have to be observed, which means that your result could be a mental result, like an answer or a decision. However, your results must be something under your control, regardless of whether the result is mental or physical.

Self-Test
Do your Results Support your Boss?

Effective people have a strong sense of duty, do the right thing at the right time, and don't need prodding or reminding.

Here are the most common expectations of your results:

1. Are you *accountable* for your results and the consequences?
2. Do you help your boss achieve his goals, no matter what?
3. Do you consistently produce excellent results?
4. Do you always do your best work?
5. Do you know all that's expected of you?
6. Do you consistently get things done the right way the first time?
7. Can you be counted on to get things done without direct supervision?
8. Do you proactively anticipate problems?
9. Are you self-correcting?
10. Do you catch errors and mistakes before your boss?
11. Do you recommend solutions to your boss?
12. Do you continuously seek ways to improve what you do?

13. Are you improving your skills through training?

14. Do you ensure your boss is the first to hear any bad news?

15. If you don't know, do you ask?

16. If you're supposed to know something but don't, do you find out and follow-through ASAP?

17. Do you contribute to your boss's meetings, activities, and events?

18. Do you cease discussion when your boss makes the final decision?

19. Do you support your boss's decisions, as your decision, especially if you disagree?

20. Do you ensure your focus and priorities reinforce your boss's?

21. Do you know your boss's intent, responsibilities, expectations, projects, goals, and standards?

22. Do you know your boss's values, priorities, and idiosyncrasies?

23. Do you have access to information sharing and processing?

24. Do you have permission to voice your honest opinion, behind closed doors, without fear of negative consequences?

25. Do you avoid last-minute surprises for your boss?

26. Do you keep the boss informed?

27. Do you anticipate and accommodate change?

28. Do you follow up and follow-through?

29. Do you know what matters most to your boss?

30. Do you ask for feedback from your boss and team members?

31. Do you manage your workload and professional development?

32. Do you manage your time, changes, and challenges well?

If you answered NO to five or more of these questions, you need to reassess your results and change what needs to be changed. Effective people take this assessment annually to demonstrate that they're *self-correcting* (Appendix G).

35
BY ASSESSING
BEHAVIOR

"If a man aspires to the highest place, it is no
dishonor to him to halt at the second."
- Cicero

How will your boss assess your behavior? Your behavior includes your competencies, skills, attitude, expertise, and proficiencies. It also includes your adherence to company values, policies, and procedures, as well as feedback from team members, customers, and suppliers. And let's not forget your personal style, manner, and approach used.

Behavior is normally measured subjectively (someone's opinion), but not always. You're expected to perform your job in a way that reflects positively on the company's standards and expectations. Your behavior is the sum of everything you say and do, as well as everything you fail to say and do.

Self-Test
Does your Behavior Support your Boss?

Effective people have a strong sense of duty, do the right thing at the right time, and don't need prodding or reminding.

Here are the most common expectations of your behavior.

1. Do you treat everyone with respect and kindness?

2. Are you *accountable* for your behavior and the consequences?

3. Do you add value to all those who help you achieve your results?

4. Do you play by the rules unless you have a good reason for not doing so?

5. Do you demonstrate a positive attitude?

6. Do you avoid gossiping and speaking badly of others unless in your boss's office, privately?

7. Are you a team player?

8. Do you fully cooperate, coordinate, and collaborate?

9. Do you stay home and call your boss if you have common signs of being sick?

10. Do you know your boss's expectations of tradition and culture?

11. Do you deal honestly with others - revealing problems and telling the whole story?

12. Do you avoid wasting your boss's time?

13. Do you maintain the standards for behavior?

14. Do you give feedback to your boss? (Chapter 10)

15. Do you refrain from making excuses? (Appendix G)

16. Do you refrain from complaining and blaming others?

17. Does your behavior reflect positively on your company?

18. Do you demonstrate *accountability* (Appendix G)?

19. Do you communicate well with customers and team members?

20. Do you adhere to all restrictions, policies, and procedures?

21. Does your behavior contribute to the stability, harmony, integrity, or cohesiveness of your team?

If you answered NO to three or more of these questions, you need to reassess your behavior and change what needs to be changed. Effective people take this assessment annually to demonstrate that they're *self-correcting* (Appendix G).

36
BY ASSESSING POTENTIAL

"We must develop the capacity to see men, not as they are at present, but as they may become."
– Thomas S. Monson

How will your boss assess your potential?

Potential is the latent qualities or abilities that may be developed and lead to future success or usefulness.

The best sales associate doesn't always make the best manager of sales associates.

In my view, your potential has more to do with character than performance.

Does the best sales associate treat those around him with respect and kindness? Measuring potential is normally done subjectively, but not always.

I like what **Roger Edwards**, *Pilat HR Solutions*, had to say about objectively assessing someone's potential by using these four factors:

- **"General intelligence:** The ability of an individual to assimilate quickly to new and complex data, make sense of it, spot themes and trends, balance hard and soft data, and make contextually significant decisions.

- **Emotional drivers:** The core drive and resilience to face the competitive world, balanced with *self-awareness, humility, agility, and the ability to learn continuously and engage others to achieve beyond their expectations.

- **Business acumen:** Understanding business and financial models, business politics, and navigating networks to achieve results.

*To learn more about *Awareness*, available at **Amazon.com,** see page 5.

- **Historic performance record:** Last year's annual performance rating isn't enough; rather, is there a sufficient record of the person facing new challenges and bringing to bear those capabilities and behaviors that enable them to succeed time and again?

It's essential to create a framework for measuring potential while considering that the future's required skills may change. This is why models that assess *self-awareness* and learning ability are becoming increasingly more important."

In the end, the most frequently used subjective assessment comes from answering this simple question,

"Putting personal relationships aside, if I were to retire tomorrow, who would I recommend as my successor and why?"

What's Character?

True character is right behavior; what you say and do when no one's around. Character is how you treat others, especially when under stress. Being a person of character is a conscious choice you make every day.

A character quality is a habit, a usual pattern or way of thinking, speaking, and acting. Like any habit, a character quality can be developed, and an undesirable quality can be eliminated by repeatedly making decisions and taking actions that reinforce character.

Character is also a sign of maturity and is reflected in how you treat others, especially your subordinates and strangers. For example, do you treat everyone with respect and kindness? Or do you play favorites and only treat those in positions of authority with respect and kindness?

Character can be developed by any combination of *motivations or by default. Of course, you're responsible for your thoughts, words, and deeds, but there may be hereditary, environmental, and training factors that have affected your character. Regardless, you're still responsible for your response to these factors and the development of good habits.

*To learn more about *Motivating,* available at **Amazon.com,** see page 5.

What are the most influential character traits?

Another good way of assessing potential come from your boss's subjective assessment of your character using these most influential *character traits:

- **Adaptable:** Are you flexible enough to see alternate solutions?

- **Loyalty:** Are you loyal to your team and your boss?

- **Judgment:** Do you make good decisions in a timely manner?

- **Moral Courage:** Do you stand up for what's right and for others?

- **Positive Attitude:** Do you add value to others?

- **Integrity:** Do you keep your promises?

- **Dependability:** Can you be counted on to consistently produce excellent results?

- **Drive:** Do you get things done without outside assistance?

- **Humility:** Do you treat others with respect and kindness?

Remember, your Legacy Story always ends the same way; you are what you leave behind!

Do you have good communication with your boss? If in doubt, ask! Get your fear and pride out of the way! If your question could embarrass your boss or others, ask privately.

*To learn more about *Character,* available at **Amazon.com,** see page 5.

This page is intentionally left blank.

37
BY LEARNING FROM
MISTAKES AND FAILURE

*"If you're not making mistakes, then you're not doing anything.
I'm positive that a doer makes mistakes."*
- John Wooden

Will you make mistakes and have failures in your lifetime? You bet lots of them. But that's how we all learn. So, how can you learn from mistakes and failure? Effective people know that the only thing that matters is what you learn for the next time.

What's Failure?

The dictionary defines failure as:

"The state or condition of not meeting a desirable or intended goal and may be viewed as the opposite of success."

Failure is a relative term. It's viewed differently depending on your situation and who's doing the viewing. For example, failure to a baseball player may be striking out, but failure to his coach might be losing the game.

In the Business World, your goals will come from your boss. Did you accomplish the goals you were assigned? Did you achieve the result you wanted? If not, why?

The only important question is, what did you learn that can make you better next time? I used to think that there was no such thing as failure (it didn't exist) as long as you never gave up. But this is only partially true and sends the wrong message.

You'll experience mistakes and failures in your life. The trick is not to let them define you.

Instead, let them Refine you and make you stronger!

The past doesn't equal the future. So learn what you need to learn and move on!

What's the difference between a failure and an unsuccessful attempt?

- **Failure** needs a substantial loss (like money, time, or reputation).

- **An Unsuccessful Attempt** means that your last attempt did not achieve the desired result.

However, if you can make another attempt, did you learn why the last attempt was unsuccessful? Do you know what changes need to be made for your next attempt to be successful? The example most often used comes from the story of **Thomas Edison** and his 10,000 attempts to create the incandescent light bulb.

Failure only exists if there's a loss.
The bigger the loss, the bigger the failure.

Just remember, *Edison* could make as many attempts as he needed until he was successful because he wasn't paying for each attempt. His investors were paying the bills. Most people don't have that luxury.

What's Failure in the Real World?

There are two types of failure which are commonly misunderstood:

- **Personal failure:** This is an unsuccessful attempt at accomplishing your personal goal and includes a:

  - ✓ **Failure to try.** This is never setting goals or never attempting to accomplish anything.

  - ✓ **Failure to keep trying.** This means that after an unsuccessful initial attempt, you failed to learn from your mistakes, make the changes needed, find a different way to get there, or make another attempt.

  - ✓ **Substantial Loss.** This is a loss of your wealth, relationships, health, character, or reputation.

- **Company failure:** This is a failure to accomplish an assigned goal, resulting in losing anything your boss couldn't afford to lose.

Let's examine what should happen BEFORE you attempt to accomplish any goal.

Before the Attempt

Step 1. What's the Risk?

Conduct a *Risk Assessment* to look for all the things that could reasonably go wrong during your attempt. Then, collaborate to assess all your safety, security, financial, and operational risk and how they can be mitigated.

Step 2. How many attempts?

If you know you'll only get one attempt, make it count! If you know you'll get more than one attempt, but not an unlimited number, then you have some risk, but how can this be mitigated? On the other hand, if you know you'll get as many attempts as you need, then the only risk is the cost of each additional attempt. Remember *Edison*?

Step 3. What's the cost?

- **Cost:** What will it cost to make this attempt (how much time, money, or effort will it take)?
- **Opportunity Costs:** What are you losing by not using other alternatives?

Step 4. What if you're wrong?

Can everyone live with an unsuccessful attempt?

Step 5. What are the benefits?

What benefits will you receive if your attempt is successful?

Step 6. Is the benefit worth the cost?

- **If Yes:** Continue to create your *Plan of Action*.

- **If No or Unsure:** Work hard to mitigate your Risk. Then, conduct another Cost/Benefit Analysis.

Step 7. What's your Assessment System?

An *Assessment System* is a series of procedures designed to measure the most critical parameters of your attempt to determine what went wrong, right, and why (Chapter 6)? How will the attempt be measured? How do you know when it's time to *pull-the-plug*?

After the Attempt

Let's examine what should happen AFTER your attempt.

Step 8. Was the attempt a complete success?

- **If Yes:** Congrats! What's next?

- **If No:** If your attempt was unsuccessful, was there a loss?

  - ✓ If there was NO loss, what did you learn, and what changes need to be made? Never give up! Just find another way to get there.

  - ✓ If there was a loss, now you have a real failure. The greater the loss, the greater the failure.

Step 9. What did you learn from your Assessment System?

- What went wrong, right, and why?

- What needs to change to make your next attempt a success?

- How will you know when it's time to *pull-the-plug*?

The lesson may have been painful, but don't throw the learning away. Mistakes and failures can be your best teacher, but only if you remember the lesson.

Now what? Well, that depends on you!

Is Failure Fatal?

"Failure is not fatal, but failure to change might be."
- John Wooden

Assuming your attempt resulted in a loss, it's not the end of your life or your career. And, sometimes, getting close is good enough. So assess what happened, what you learned, and get *back-in-the-game!*

Never give up! Just find another way to get there.

Never Stop Learning!

Can you achieve Success without Failure?

"If things are not failing, you are not innovating enough."
- Elon Musk

For all of *Elon Musk's* success, he has experienced an equal amount of failure. Whatever future success he achieves will most likely be accompanied by more failure.

Here are three times *Elon Musk* failed:

1. Once, he couldn't get a CEO job to save his life.

When *Zip2* began attracting investors, they stripped him of his role as Chairman. Musk's idea of leadership in the 1990s was to stay late and rewrite code, believing his employees were incompetent. He failed to see how publicly berating his employees might make them less productive.

2. He has crashed more than his share of rockets.

His career serves as ample proof that the first step to success is a whole bunch of failures. Until April 8, 2016, **SpaceX** managed the first of three consecutive successful landings. Then, unfortunately, the results in June resulted in four rocket launches in a row ending in flames.

3. He has never delivered a car on time.

Tesla revealed that it built only 260 Model 3 vehicles, instead of the promised 1,500, with no chance of making the claimed initial 5,000 by the end of the year. Shipments were initially expected to begin in 2013, yet the first cars didn't ship until late 2015.

By comparison, it took *Amazon* more than 14 years to make as much profit as it produced the previous quarter. *Amazon* consistently lost money for its first several years as a public company.

Lessons Learned: Constantly seek criticism and feedback; it's as good as gold! Never give up. Just find another way to get there.

"Being an entrepreneur starting up is like eating glass and staring into the abyss of death."
- Unknown

This page is intentionally left blank.

38
BY DEMONSTRATING
GOOD JUDGMENT

"Experience is simply the name we give our mistakes."
- Oscar Wilde

In your attempt to save time, do you rush and make snap decisions without considering the consequences?

Good judgment is your ability to bring together reason and wisdom to analyze a situation, explore your options, select a course of action, and take action.

Good judgment isn't about being smart or about making good decisions.

The essence of good judgment is about learning from past mistakes.

It's about using your *Assessment Systems* (Chapter 6) to ensure you don't repeat the same mistakes and increase the probability of success of your next attempt.

Judgment is less about getting it right and more about what it takes to learn what went wrong.

Some of your decisions will result in *Unintended Consequences*. To add to this uncertainty, you'll soon discover that your decisions aren't always about what's good or bad. Often, they're about choosing between good, better, and best. All decisions have consequences, which you won't see in advance. But experience teaches that they'll come due someday.

Where do good decisions come from?

Good decisions don't happen by accident.

- Good decisions come from good judgment.
- Good judgment comes from failure.
- Failure comes from mistakes.
- Mistakes come from bad decisions.

- Bad decisions come from bad judgment.
- Bad judgment comes from a lack of experience.
- Lack of experience comes from:
  - ✓ Having little time invested in the job.
  - ✓ Not learning from your mistakes.
  - ✓ Not learning from the mistakes of others.
  - ✓ Making quick decisions when you have more time.
  - ✓ A failure to venture outside your comfort zone.

Mistakes, as long as you learn from them,
are the building blocks of greatness.

How can you learn from the mistakes of others?

Learning from the mistakes of others only happens if you're paying attention. The truth is that anyone can cut their learning curve and gain years of valuable experience by using this simple principle:

There are only two ways to learn anything in life, either
by trial and error or by modeling the best practices.

While it's important to learn from your mistakes, it's a lot easier to learn from the mistakes of others.

How can Modeling help you?

Experience is the toughest teacher because it gives
the test first and the knowledge second.

Modeling a better teacher because it gives you the knowledge, so you're better prepared for the test.

Modeling is the process of learning from those
who've already achieved success.

It also means learning by copying the behavior of those who've already experienced the mistakes and failures on their journey to success (Chapter 37). You can avoid the same mistakes and failures by learning, applying, and sharing what you'll learn here. Each new skill learned builds on the previous, and the compound effect is career-changing.

39

BY KNOWING WHEN TO
ACT, WAIT OR WALK AWAY

"You got to know when to hold 'em. Know when to fold 'em.
Know when to walk away and know when to run."
- Kenny Rogers, The Gambler.

When faced with a problem, how do you know what to do? For every problem you'll face, you'll normally have three choices of how to respond:

You can act, wait, or walk away.

When faced with a problem, can't you just do nothing? Sure. Think about it. You have this option every time you're faced with a problem. Do some problems sometimes correct themselves by doing nothing? Yes. Do some problems get worse by taking action rather than doing nothing? You bet!

Remember, doing nothing is deciding by default.

Are there some problems that are better left alone? Sure. Just ask any Fire-fighter. Most of the time, all they can do is contain the fire and just let it burn itself out; let it *burn-to-the-ground*. If you feel this is your best choice, among all the choices you have at the time, then do nothing – let it burn-to-the-ground

However, doing nothing and waiting
are two different options.

When faced with any problem, use these steps to guide your response.

Step 1: Should I Act NOW?

Before deciding, answer these questions?

- Can this problem be resolved by calling 911? If Yes, call!

- Will acting now save lives or avoid further damage?

    ✓ If Yes, take *Immediate Action* (Appendix B).

    ✓ If No to both questions, continue to Step 2.

Step 2: Is this my problem?

Is this my problem or someone else's?

- Who has the most to gain or lose from its resolution?

- Who's affected by this problem?

If this problem isn't your problem, why are you trying to solve it? Just report it to your boss and walk away. If this is your problem, continue to the next step.

Step 3: Should I act now or wait?

How urgent is this problem?

- How important or urgent is this problem and why?

- What must happen before I'm forced to act?

- What are the consequences if this problem remains unresolved?

- What's the downside of waiting?

How much time do I have?

- How long do I have before this problem becomes a crisis?

- How long do I have before I'm forced to act?

- When's it too late to act?

Based on your answers to the above questions, use the *Decision Support Template* below to guide your decision.

Here's an example of a *Decision Support Template*: Time vs. Urgency.

Decision Support Matrix		Time to Decide?	
		Little Time	Enough Time
Urgency?	Urgent	1	2
	Not Urgent	3	4

Here's what the numbers mean:

1. If this problem is urgent and you have little time to decide, take *Immediate Action* (Appendix B) and develop a mental *Plan of Action* before acting (Appendix A). See CONPLAN 1.

2. If this problem is urgent and you have enough time, take Step 4. Prepare to act after completing your *Plan of Action*. Keep your boss informed. See CONPLAN 2.

3. If this problem isn't urgent and you have little time to decide, wait, continue to monitor the situation, create your *Plan of Action*, and keep your boss informed. See CONPLAN 3.

4. If this problem isn't urgent and you have enough time to act, continue to monitor the situation, create your *Plan of Action*, and update your boss. See CONPLAN 4.

Also, document what happened, when, and who took what action to resolve the problem for investigative or legal purposes later.

Step 4: Create your Plan of Action.

See Appendix A.

Note: You're responsible for anticipating your work's consequences and effects BEFORE deciding (Chapter 22).

Other Things to Consider

When's the best time to decide?

> *"The key is not to make quick decisions,*
> *but to make timely decisions."*
> *- Colin Powell*

Do you have to make the decision right now? This classic answer is usually, No! This is rarely necessary. Resist the impulse of making a snap decision when there's no need to do so. Normally, you'll have sufficient time to decide.

A good rule of thumb is to decide after acquiring **40-70%** of the information you need. Mistakes, as long as you learn from them, are the building blocks of greatness. If it turns out bad, adjust, and remember what you've learned for next time.

Who's the Best Person to decide?

First, the boss decides! Or, at least, the boss should take responsibility and ownership of his team's decisions, especially if it turns out bad. Ask members for their input before you decide. Also, if the decision affects everyone in your team, why can't all members be given a chance to concur or non-concur with reasons (Chapter 23)?

Does the Best Decision always produce the Best Outcome?

There's a big difference between your decision and the result or outcome of your decision. You could be the most experienced decision-maker on the planet, and you could make the best decision, but there's no guarantee that your problem will be resolved or the best outcome will be achieved. You can actually make a good decision, and the results could still be bad. The situation and facts available when you first decided could (and probably will) change over time. What was good today could turn out to be bad tomorrow.

Do you need your Boss's Approval?

Have you ever been in a situation where you were waiting for your boss's approval? Why are you asking for approval if the problem is internal, doesn't require additional resources you don't have, and isn't in conflict with any internal standards? Of course, that's what your boss is paying you to do. But do let him know.

Sometimes it's easier to ask forgiveness than permission.

Or, if you're in doubt, tell your boss when you'll be making your decision (like the end of the week), and if you don't hear from him before that time, you'll be moving forward. Don't forget to assess the consequences and effects of your actions.

What if a Direct Reports recommends a change?

One of the best bosses I ever worked with once said,

> **"If I can't give you a good reason not to
> make the change; I'll approve it."**

Yes, they still had to create a *Decision Paper* (Appendix C), build consensus with the team (Chapter 23), and present it to the team for a final discussion before approval. However, this gave the team the freedom they needed to make things better.

40
BY INSPECTING
WHAT YOU EXPECT

"When performance is measured, performance improves.
When performance is measured and reported,
the rate of improvement accelerates."
- Thomas S. Monson

How do you determine if your team's results meet the expected standards? While systems can assist in assessing performance, effective people know that their personal presence remains the most effective tool for assessing their members, teams, and systems.

Inspections allow you to see and be seen, test systems, and find your best members. They also help you reinforce your purpose, direction, and goals. And let's not forget, inspections help you identify strengths and weaknesses.

Inspecting means visiting and checking (members, equipment, and resources to ensure organizational standards are being met). Inspecting also means paying attention, asking questions, getting involved, knowing what is going on, and being there.

What must be done before inspecting?

Before inspecting, you need to know the organization's performance standards (behavior), what is expected (results), the Standards of Safety, Security, Property Accountability, and the *Health and Welfare* of your team, and how to make corrections.

As the boss, you should always be

inspecting what you expect!

Conducting an inspection is nothing more than knowing the standards and paying attention while observing your members and noting discrepancies and successes. So, roll up your sleeves and get involved! Never underestimate the power of your presence.

Effective people are upfront and visible to their members to inspire confidence and trust. Your absence solicits just the opposite. Get out there!

Let your members see you. Interact, get involved, and make a difference by your presence. Find out how they're doing and help them resolve their problems.

Show a sincere interest in them as human beings. This is the only way you'll ever know what's going on. For example, effective people conduct inspections in business as part of their risk management and quality assurance programs. But, without a good inspection program, even effective people experience how quickly things can go wrong.

Here are the most important steps to create an effective inspection program.

Step 1. What should you be Inspecting?

With the help of your team, assess all the things that are most important to you and your team's ability to consistently produce excellent results. For example, let's assume that your team has identified 16 Most Important Things (MIT) critical to the consistent production of excellent results. Furthermore, these 16 MITs are at 16 different locations.

Step 2. Where should you be Inspecting?

Write each MIT on a 3 x 5 card and place these 16 cards into an envelope labeled, "Inspect Today." Then, every day select one 3 x 5 card from the "Inspect Today" envelope and conduct an unannounced inspection. When finished, note the date and results on the 3 x 5 card and place it into a second envelope labeled, "Done." When the "Inspect Today" envelope is empty, repeat this process.

Step 3. When should you be Inspecting?

Unannounced inspections are more effective than scheduled inspections because if your members know when you're coming, they may only "clean-up-their-act." After all, they knew you were coming. On the other hand, if you show up at random, unscheduled, you will find your members doing what they usually do.

You don't want them wasting their time preparing for your visit. Also, if you find a mess when you arrive, that's okay; life isn't perfect. Just schedule a *Re-Inspection* in a few days. And, if you're lucky enough to have a *Staff*, this is what they should be doing on your behalf – with the results provided to you.

Step 4. What should you do during your visits?

Let's assume that you're visiting a Direct Report that has five Direct Reports reporting to him. When you visit, start with a private conversation with your Direct Report and attempt to answer these questions:

- Did you find what you expected? Is he present and doing what you expected? If absent, who's *In Charge*?

- Does he know where his members are and what they're doing?

- What problems does he usually have, and how does he resolve them?

- Does he have what he needs to do his job? Are the working conditions reasonable and safe?

- What are the most difficult tasks he and his team must perform?

- When are the most stressful times of the day, week, month, or year and why?

- Is it secure (high dollar items, marked, inventoried, serviceable, cared for, stored properly) from theft and damage?

- Is he keeping track of the right things? Are he and his team members trained to do their job?

- How do his team members get trained? Is he taking care of his members?

- How can you help him?

Have your Direct Report lead you through their MIT's. Based on everything you see, is he and his team following the standards set by the company? Document any recommendations, corrections, or follow-through needed.

Here's a Great Story:

One day in May, when Tom first met one of his five Electric Power Line Crews for the first time, he asked the Team Leader, "When's the most stressful time of the year and why?" He answered, "After the first major winter snowstorm." He explained that the stress came from all the tree branches falling and taking out power lines.

Tom pulled out his notebook to record this answer. The other four teams had the same response. So a few days later, Tom asked his five Team Leaders, "How can we avoid or reduce this problem every year?" The first answer was to cut down all the trees - which homeowners would never agree to do.

Another Team Leader said, "Why don't we just trim the tree branches that are above or near the power lines?" Tom agreed and got the go-ahead from his boss, and in late August, they began to systematically trim all branches over or near power lines. The next winter, the number of power lines downed by tree branches reduced by 90%.

Most important: If you want to send the *Powerful Message*, <u>write things down</u>. Seriously, put your devices away, pull out your 3 X 5 cards from your pocket, and start writing. And, let them see you writing. Record their name. Later, if you said you'd help, *Follow-through* to deliver what you said you would to let him know you didn't forget him even if you can't help, at least *Follow-through* and tell him why.

Biggest Mistakes: The biggest mistakes bosses make when inspecting include inspecting things that members didn't expect, inspecting without the Direct Report, only visiting when things go wrong, not knowing the standards, changing standards-surprising people, not correcting what needs to be corrected, and not providing encouragement and praise for the good.

Reinspecting: If your inspection uncovers several deficiencies, give the Direct Report a week to make the corrections, and conduct a scheduled reinspection on only those deficient items.

Understanding how to conduct an inspection and reinspection will help you assess the effectiveness of your members, teams, and systems.

APPENDIX A:
CREATE A PLAN OF ACTION

Here's a great checklist to use when creating your next *Plan of Action*.

OBJECTIVE (Who, What, Where, When, and Why?)

- What's my access to sources of info, and who's this project for?
- Where is this project being conducted?
- Why is this project being done?
- How important is this project, and to whom is it important?
- How will success be measured, and who will measure it?
- What's the requirement, scope, and complexity of work?
- What's the limit of my authority (decisions, delegate, spend $, hire, and fire)?
- Does someone with authority approve this?
- When does this project start and end?
- What's the most important task for this project to be a success?
- Who has done this task before, and what were their problems, consequences, and effects?
- What must be ordered or started now?

METHODS

- How should we do it? What are all our options, which is best?
- What needs to happen during the four phases of this project?
- What're all the tasks involved, and who are responsible for performing each task (Key Player)?
- What must be done before, during, and after the project?
- What specific instructions do we have for those delegated a task?
- How many are expected to attend or are affected by this?
- What're our restrictions (can't do) and imperatives (must do)?
- Who has done this or a similar type of project before?
- How will this project be advertised or promoted?
- What are my responsibilities, expectations, duties, constraints, authority, and standards?
- Who're the most important people to talk to right now?
- What're the consequences if this turns out unsuccessful?

- *Planning backward from today, when are the Planning, Preparing, Executing, and Assessment Phases?
- When's the *Backbriefing?*
- What's the *Project Update Briefing* schedule?
- Which *Preventive Actions* must be done during each phase?
- How long will each task take, and what's the best sequence of these tasks and *Preventive Actions*?
- Which tasks can't start or finish without another task starting or ending? (Dependent tasks)
- Which task needs to be started right now?
- What's the detailed schedule, program, and calendar?
- When's the rehearsal, and what will be rehearsed?
- What else is going on in the company or *community at the same time? What happened last year at this time?

*Do you really want your project to go on at the same time as Spring Break, the Superbowl, or a Presidential Election Voting Day?

RESOURCES

- What resources are most important for the success of this project?
- How much of each resource is needed, when, and where?
- Who's responsible (Key Player) for providing these resources?
- When's the latest time we need these resources delivered?
- Who's paying for this, and what must be ordered now?
- What skills, attitudes, or knowledge are needed, and who has the skills we need?
- Any special needs for safety, security, sanitation, disabilities?
- What're our *Shortfalls* (anything you need to complete a project that you don't have)?
- How much money can we spend? What's our Budget?

*To learn more about **Planning**, available at **Amazon.com,** see page 5.

- What do we need to know but don't?
- What do we know for sure, but the answer is unsatisfactory or unacceptable?
- What are our shortfalls, which are things we need but don't have?
- What are all the questions, unknowns, concerns, shortfalls, obstacles, or problems that could slow or stop your progress?
- Who has done this type of work before, and what were their problems, consequences, and effects?
- What are we forgetting to do?

Also, in Appendix E, you'll find a copy of my personal checklist called *"Don't Forget Nothin,"* which I've compiled over my lifetime as a way of remembering all the things I should consider when planning anything.

RISK (Chapters 26-28)

- **Physical: (Injury, Illness, or Death)**
  - ✓ Have we inspected the site for anything that could cause injury, illness, accident, or death?
  - ✓ Have we inspected for sanitation and access for those with disabilities?

- **Security: (Cyber and Physical)**
  - ✓ For Cybersecurity: What could cause a data breach, loss of personal info or intellectual property, or a disruption of services?
  - ✓ For Physical Security: What could cause unauthorized access leading to theft, fraud, waste, abuse, or property damage?

- **Financial:**
  - ✓ What could cause financial loss or property damage?
  - ✓ What insurance do we need, and is it *in-force*?

- **Operational:**
  See Chapter 26: Risk Assessment

This page is intentionally left blank.

B
TAKE
IMMEDIATE ACTION

How do you respond to unanticipated bad situations?

Immediate Action is a proactive eight-step process used to react to any bad situation that could cause a work stoppage, property damage, a security breach, or physical injury.

Let's drill down on the eight steps of the *Immediate Action* process.

Step 1. Assess the Situation.

Either be *on-the-scene* or in communication with someone on the ground. Assess the situation based on the facts.

Step 2. Notify Emergency Services and your boss.

If needed, call 911, and call your boss to tell him what you know.

Step 3. Consider your Options.

Look around. What's available for you to use? What should be done to stabilize the situation? What are your options? If time permits, collaborate with others.

Step 4. Select the Best Option.

Select the best option, and if time permits, achieve consensus with those around you.

Step 5. Create a Plan of Action.

Create a quick mental *Plan of Action*. What's the first step? What's the second, and so forth?

Step 6. Take Decisive Action.

Using what's available, *take-charge*, and give new instructions to others. Supervise their actions.

Step 7. Reassess the Situation.

What, if anything, has changed? Did the situation stabilize, or was the problem resolved? If Yes, move to Step 8. If NO, repeat this process.

Step 8. Call your boss.

Keep your boss informed. Explain what happened, what caused it, and what you recommend be done to ensure this never happens again. Sounds pretty easy, right? Well, let's see how it's done in the real world.

True Story

At 9 AM, two days before his company's annual Team Building Session, Bob, the Project Manager, conducted his final site inspection of the resort and was astonished by what he saw. He tried to pull into the resort, blocked by construction vehicles tearing up the parking lot. This was a disaster for Bob because he had 50 Senior Executives flying in from all over the country for this session. Fortunately, Bob knew how to take Immediate Action.

Step 1. Assess the Situation.

Bob didn't panic. He assessed the situation, took photos with his cell phone, spoke with the resort manager, and learned that a major water main had broken, which meant that the resort had no water. Bob also talked to the on-site construction manager and learned that the water main could not be repaired for another week.

Step 2. Call Emergency Services and your boss.

At 9:30 AM: Since there was no need to call 911, Bob called his boss and appraised him of the situation.

Step 3. Consider your options.

At 10 AM, Bob called a meeting of all Key Players at company headquarters to collaborate to find the best solution. Bob asked one Key Player to find another venue that could accommodate 50 people.

By 11 AM, a new venue had been found, but it was 27 miles from the airport. One problem was solved, but it created another. How will all attendees get from the airport to the resort? Someone asked, can't they just catch a cab or just rent a car at the airport? For 50 people to catch a cab or rent a car would be way too expensive.

Step 4. Select the best option.

Then someone suggested that they rent a fleet of shuttle vehicles with drivers to transport all attendees from the airport to the resort and back. They all agreed that this was the best solution.

Step 5. Create a Plan of Action.

Together they created a Plan of Action to use shuttle vehicles to accomplish the objective.

Step 6. Take Decisive Action.

Bob issued new instructions to all Key Players and supervised their actions. He assigned one Key Player to contact all attendees to let them know what happened and look for company signs at the airport directing them to shuttle vehicles rather than taking a cab or renting a vehicle. Bob also asked a second Key Player to identify and contract a shuttle company to transport all attendees. Finally, he asked everyone to meet again at 5 PM to share the status of their new assignments.

Step 7. Reassess the Situation.

At 5 PM that afternoon, Bob met with all Key Players to ensure everything was ready to move forward with a fleet of shuttle vehicles.

Step 8. Report to your boss.

At 6 PM, Bob called his boss and informed him that the problem was resolved by selecting a new site and renting a fleet of shuttle vans to drive all attendees from the airport to the hotel and back. There was no reason to recommend what needed to be done to ensure this didn't happen again. The Team Building Session went on without any further problems and turned out to be a great success.

Bob looked defeat in the eye and refused to give up,

"Snatching Victory from the Jaws of Defeat."

And you can do the same!

This page is intentionally left blank.

C
CREATE A
DECISION PAPER

How do you create a convincing document to persuade someone to spend the money needed to move your work forward? Sometimes you'll need resources that you don't have, like people, equipment, or facilities, to solve a problem – which means spending money. When this happens, you'll need the DM's approval before moving forward.

To persuade anyone to accept your recommendation, you'll need a well-written *Decision Paper,* and here's a great format.

What's the best format to use to create a Decision Paper?

1. Subject. Briefly state the subject.

2. Problem. State the problem in one sentence.

3. Recommendation. State the recommended solution in one sentence.

4. Benefits: State the expected benefits of this recommendation.

5. Key Player Comments.

A Key Player is anyone whose opinion would matter to the Decision-Maker or anyone who'll be required to support the recommendation if approved. You'll need to *Staff* your paper through all Key Players for their concurrence or non-concurrence with comments (Chapter 23). Once comments are returned, create a table showing which Key Players concurred or non-concurred with their reasons.

6. Discussion. Explain why you're recommending this solution by answering these questions.

- **What were all the solutions you considered?** Then, attach all the solutions you considered with all the Advantages and Disadvantages.

- **Why did you select this solution?**

- **What's the cost and who should pay?**

- **What's the Risk?** How probable is this risk, how severe will it be, and how can it be mitigated (Chapters 26-28). If a *Contingency Plan* is needed, add it as an enclosure (Chapter 30).

- **How long will it take, and when should it be started?**

- **How long do we have before this problem becomes a crisis?**

- **What are the consequences and effects of this recommendation?** *Unintended Consequences* are outcomes that are not expected from your project. *2nd and 3rd Order Effects* deal with how your project affects others, like those in your company or your suppliers (Chapter 22).

- **What are the *Unresolved Issues*?** Attach a list of all the questions, unknowns, concerns, shortfalls, obstacles, and problems that could slow or stop your progress (Chapter 21).

- **What are all the Facts and Assumptions?** Attach a list of all the facts and assumptions you used (Appendix D).

When your paper is finished, give a Decision Briefing or provide a hard copy to the DM to gain approval. If you choose this option, ensure your paper is no more than two pages in length, with all the supporting documents attached as enclosures.

What's a Business Case?

A *Decision Paper* is also known as a *Business Case*, which is the justification to convince a Decision-Maker to accept a proposal.

A Business Case is a document that captures the reasons for initiating an action.

The logic is that whenever resources are consumed, they should support a specific business need. For example, it could be a software upgrade needed to improve system performance. The "business case" is that a software upgrade would improve customer satisfaction, require less task processing time, or reduce system maintenance costs. A compelling business case should capture both the quantifiable and non-quantifiable characteristics of the proposed action.

Creating a *Decision Paper* or a *Business Case* is a great way to convince your boss to accept your recommendation and enhance your credibility.

D
GATHER
ASSUMPTIONS AND FACTS

Do you know how to gather all the assumptions, facts, and the truth needed to persuade others to support you to enhance your probability of success?

By identifying the Assumptions

An ASSUMPTION is information accepted as true in the absence of facts.

However, acceptable assumptions must pass two tests.

- They must be **VALID**, which means that they're likely to be true.

- They must be **NECESSARY**, which means that they're essential to moving the work forward.

If the process can continue without the assumption, discard it. If the assumption is both valid and necessary, then treat it as a fact. Effective people continually seek to confirm their assumptions by testing. For example, if you assume that the weather won't be a problem for your company's outdoor picnic, you better have a *Contingency Plan* - just in case. Better yet, if it rains and you've reserved an outdoor picnic site with overhead cover, now you're the hero of the day.

You know the old saying about assumptions, right?

Whenever you assume anything, you risk making an 'ass' out of 'u' and 'me.'

People aren't mind readers. Never assume that all understand your expectations. It doesn't matter how much experience you have or how long you've been in your position. If you feel there's a chance of a misunderstanding, clarify all your expectations.

Here's an example:

"As an executive coach, one of my C-level clients shared with me his disappointment with a new VP he recently hired. He explained that he told his new VP that he expected him to really "step up" and get us to "the next level" in sales. However, after six months, he and his sales team had not met his expectations.

I asked him, "Have you defined what 'stepping up' and 'getting to the next level' mean?" My client responded, "No, why would I? With his experience, he should know what I mean." Ops!

What's an Unconscious Assumption?

Sometimes assumptions are made unconsciously. So, be careful!

Here's an example:

Bob walked into a Problem-Solving Session where one of his Direct Reports, with his entire team, tried to select the BEST vendor from two similar companies. As the process was almost over, Bob asked, "What assumptions are you making here?" Then, after a long silence, he asked the question again.

One person said, "None, we don't need any." To which Bob said, "Are you sure? Since I only see two vendors you're considering, aren't you assuming that there are only two companies that we could potentially hire to solve this problem? Are you all certain this assumption is correct?

And, what's the effect if later this assumption proves to be incorrect? What happens later when we find out that there was a third company that could have solved our problem faster and at half the cost?" Again, there was a long silence. The group had assumed there were only two potential companies, and they were wrong.

What assumptions are you making unconsciously, and what are the effects on the project if these assumptions turn out to be wrong? What's your *Contingency Plan*?

Always Test your Assumptions and Vet your Facts!

How can you identify all your assumptions?

To help identify your assumptions, answer these questions:

- What do I hope is true or necessary for my document to be valid?

- What assumptions are needed to move the work forward?

- What assumptions am I making unconsciously?

- If my assumption becomes false, what's my *Contingency Plan* (Chapter 30)?

By identifying the Facts

A FACT is verifiable or vetted information.

Always separate facts from opinion or speculation. According to **Colin Powell**, in his book, *It Worked for Me*, you need good information to make good decisions. Verifiable information can change over time and may not tell the whole story. So, be careful! Also, verifiable or vetted facts that come with these qualifiers should make you nervous:

"In my best judgment," or "As far as I know,"
or "As best as I can tell."

Here are the most important questions you need to answer:

What do you know? How do you know for sure?
What do you need to know?

What do you think? What's your best hunch?
What's your intuition telling you?

Always distinguish the difference. You're looking for *ground-truth*, first-hand info from people closest to the issue. The best facts are current, from a reliable source, and first-hand information rather than hearsay.

In solving any problem, you must uncover the root cause - the truth. The dictionary defines truth as *"that which is true or in accordance with fact or reality."* Because of this, most people believe that all facts are true, but they're not. They're related but different. Facts can lead you to the truth, but they can also mislead you. This is because facts are what happened, while the truth is HOW and WHY it happened.

And here are a few examples.

> **Fact:** Mary was my best student. But the truth is that Mary was my only student.

> **Fact:** Sam sold nothing in May. However, the truth is that Sam was on vacation in May.

Facts without context can be misleading, and like statistics, they can be manipulated to prove or disprove just about anything. Facts can't speak for themselves. Someone else must speak for them.

Remember, nothing has meaning other than the meaning you give it. So, be careful!

What's Objective Truth?

> *"One of the greatest challenges in this world is to know enough about a subject to think your right, but not enough about the subject to know your wrong."*

I learned from **Neal deGrasse Tyson's** *Master Class* the three categories of truth: personal, political, and objective. Objective truth is truth no matter what happens and is the truth that shapes our understanding of the universe.

> *"We all have susceptibility to bias. The internet is evidence of bias. And you're going to use it as evidence to prove that you're correct? No!!!"*

E
"DON'T FORGIT NOTHIN"

Here are the most important things to consider before your next project:

- **Communications:** Do you have direct communication with your Key Players via cell phone or 2-way radios with backup batteries and chargers? Does everyone have a list of each other's phone numbers? What if they're not near their cell phone when you call (or are on another call)?

- **Fun:** Laughter, humor, music, breaks, snacks, games, awards, recognition, surprises, and prizes.

- **Getting attendees involved:** How can you put attendees to work? Have them physically do simulations, problem-solving, breakout sessions, circuit training, seminars, workshops, round-robin stations, role-playing, practical exercises, competition, or small group discussions.

- **Headquarters:** Is there a known location at the event or activity, with a dedicated phone number that's open 24/7 that tracks attendance, safety, and first aid. Do they have a vehicle, driver, and map to the nearest hospital?

- **Life Support:** How will the participants be physically sustained (includes food, drink, snacks, ice, communications, lodging (if overnight), transportation, hygiene, toilets, electricity, cooking, refrigeration, liability insurance, sanitation (hand sanitizer, toilet paper), overhead shelter (if it rains), trash containers, and trash collection and removal). The longer the time and distance from home base, the more complicated the life support becomes.

- **Other:** Parking, access for delivery vehicles, traffic flow, who tracks who's there and who's not? Do you have a backup location in case of bad weather? Did you delegate all these tasks? Do you have consensus from all Key Players?

- **Pre-work:** Do you want the participants to do something before the event and bring it with them? Do they need to review a read-ahead packet? If so, provide it in advance.

- **Program Support:** Audio and visual aids, handouts, loud-speaker, music, surveys, or backup generators?

- **Promotion:** How can you best advertise the event or activity that creates interest and anticipation? What's in it for them? What would make members want to attend? How will you communicate this to all invitees?

- **Quality Control (Assessment):** IPRs, AARs, meetings, deliverables, accountability, surveys, Contingency and Mitigation Plans, Project Updates, metrics, milestones, Timetables, and achieving consensus?

- **Rehearsals:** What do you need to see before you start? Do you need to practice, preview, or rehearse anything before the event or activity? Who's reviewing documents to see if they make sense and are correct?

- **Safety and Medical:** What if someone gets hurt? Do you need first aid kits, defibrillators, life jackets (if around water), and fire extinguishers? Are there any other hazards (like holes, cliffs, water, or any way anyone could get hurt)? How can you mitigate this risk? Do you need members trained in CPR and first aid? How about Bee stings (EpiPen® need a prescription), bug spray, location of the nearest hospital, vehicle designated to transport, maps to hospital, cell phones with 911 capabilities, and an ambulance needed on the site?

- **Schedule or Program:** Is there ample time built into the program for all to have fun and do something meaningful instead of just sitting there? How about a mixer (with name tags) so members can get to meet and know each other?

- **Search Plan:** What happens when someone is reported "missing," especially if away from the company's property?

- **Security:** Are chaperones, guards, police, crowd and traffic control, or checkers needed? Cell phones (with chargers/extra batteries), cameras, and phone# available? Are metal detectors needed to check for weapons?

- **Site Transition:** Site problems also include the poor scheduling of other units before and after your scheduled time. The concern here is that the previous unit may not be cleared of the site before you try to set-up.

- And this includes your departure at the end of your project before the next unit attempts to move in. Additionally, many units try to pre-stage and move supplies and equipment the night before the project. So make sure you know who'll be there before you and who is coming in after you to ensure a smooth handoff.

- **Small Children:** Children are a special challenge because they're so mobile and seem to find their way, unsupervised, into places where they could potentially get hurt. If there's water, you'll need life vests, lifeguards, and the like. If there's a fire or anything hot, or vehicle traffic, wells, or cliffs - get the idea?

- **Time:** What are the start and end times? What else is going on around the selected site during this time? What else is going on in the lives of those assigned to perform certain activities like graduations, summer vacations, or the Super Bowl? Hint? What happened last year at the same time and place? What's your *Contingency Plan*?

Note: You may not need all these reminders for your next project, but it's a nice checklist to add to your toolbox.

What are you forgetting?

This page is intentionally left blank.

F
TRACK
ALL THE MOVING PARTS

Do you know how to keep track of all your moving parts to ensure that nothing *falls-through-the-cracks* to enhance your probability of success?

"Tracking" means keeping a paper or digital trail (documenting) of the most important things that keep changing.

How do you keep track of all the things that are critical to your work? Effective people know that there are many " moving parts " in business, and many lose their way - unless someone tracks them.

Here are several ways to keep track of your most important "moving parts."

By Tracking Assignments

Assignments come in two types; Assignments *Accepted* from others and Assignments *Made* to others.

Here's an example of an *Assignments Tracking Form.*

Assignments Accepted					Assignments Made			
Date	From	Action Item	DL	To	Date	DL	Checked	Status
11 May	Boss	ABC Report	19 Jun	Sue	12 May	17 Jun	2 Jun	OS

Notice that this table tracks the assignments *accepted* from others (boss) and the assignments *made* to others. It's also a good idea to assign the *Action Item* to a Direct Report (Sue), with her deadline (DL) being a few days before your boss's deadline. This way, you have some *slack time* built in just in case something goes wrong.

For example, using this table, if your boss wants his assignment completed on May 19th, assign your Direct Report (Sue) a deadline of May 17th. This is your record of all assignments *made* for future meetings.

You can also create an *Assignment Tracking Form* for each Direct Report to use during your internal meetings. The most important thing to remember is never to trust your memory. Always document everything you've asked a Direct Report to do and add a deadline.

By Tracking Changes

Have you ever been frustrated with last-minute changes to a project? Have you ever tried to communicate a change to all Key Players, but 10% didn't get the word? Plans change, so be flexible! Make sure all Key Players know about all changes. Keep a record of who was told what, when, and how. It will come in handy later. Keep track of everyone who received the changes. Record and review these changes during your meetings.

Here's an example of a *Change Notification List*.

Change List for: _____Project (As of Aug 21, 20XX)				
Date	What Changed?	Originator?	Recipient?	How sent?
May 4	Add 12 to headcount	Bill	John	Phone
May 5	Next meeting 10 AM, not 9 AM.	Joe	Sam	Face-to-face

Notice that this table tracks the Originator or the source of the change, the Recipient or who was told about the change, and the How Sent or how the message was communicated.

If it's important or time-sensitive, don't use email. Many people fail to read their email for days, if at all. Many others misunderstand their email. The best means of communicating is *face-to-face* (the second is on the phone). Then, follow-through with a detailed email. Don't use email as your primary means of *communication. Who else needs to know this info? Act on that answer!

*To learn more about **Communicating**, available at **Amazon.com,** see page 5.

By Tracking Unresolved Issues

Track all Unresolved Issues, including any question, unknown, concern, shortfall, obstacle, or problem that could slow or stop your progress (Chapter 21). Each issue can only be eliminated when it's both "known for certain" and "acceptable to you." If you fail to keep track of all the moving parts, you'll be known as someone who doesn't have their *act together.

*To learn more about *Organizing,* available at **Amazon.com,** see page 5.

By Tracking Everything Else

Here are a few other things you should keep tracking of as well:

- **Time:** Calendar, meetings, Timetables, Preventive Actions, and absenteeism.
- **Budget:** Is your money being spent wisely? Are you over budget?
- **Focus:** What's your Focus? What are your top three priorities? Do your members know?
- **Goals:** What are your goals and your boss's goals?
- **Sensitive items:** What is proprietary or of high dollar value?
- **Earned Time Off:** Are members taking vacations or time off?
- **Loyal Service:** Celebrate the date each member joined your unit.
- **Birthdays:** Celebrate - "I'm so glad you were born!"
- **FAQ Site:** Your Purpose, Direction, and Serving Philosophy
- **Dashboards:** Telling how your unit or projects are doing.
- **Outstanding Requisitions:** What do we have on order?
- **Recognition program:** Who recognized, when, and why?
- **Upcoming Reports and Deadlines:** To avoid surprises and crisis management.

Note: This is why it's nice to have a #2 Person to help keep track of all Long-Term and Short-Term Extra Duty Assignments (like those listed above). Here, your #2 Person can delegate specific tasks to different team members to track and report the results to you monthly or quarterly.

This page is intentionally left blank.

G
ASSESS YOUR ACCOUNTABILITY

Do you know what to do when your boss finds something wrong with your work?

Accountability is the acceptance of responsibility for your actions and in-actions and the obligation to report, explain, and be answerable for any adverse consequences.

Accountability is often confused with responsibility. They're related but different. *Accountability* is normally not a problem - until something goes wrong.

For example, if something goes wrong within your area of responsibility, you'll get the chance to explain what happened to your boss, and maybe his boss. Sometimes, depending on the severity of the problem, your boss won't be happy with you and may treat you badly.

Most people don't understand that, yes, responsibility and *accountability* go together; they're part of the same iceberg.

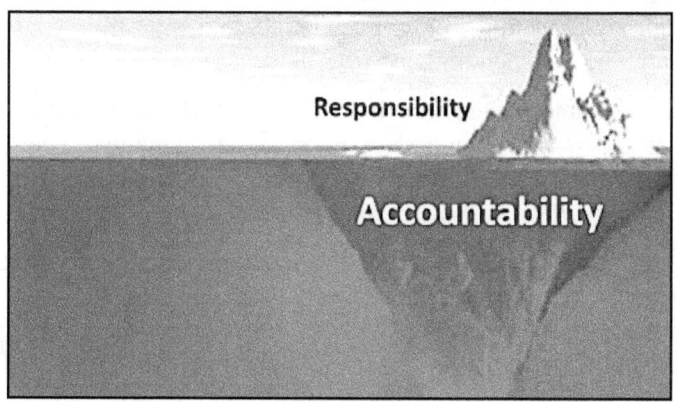

However, you can't see the *accountability* part of the iceberg because it lies hidden beneath the surface until something goes wrong.

What should you do when things go wrong?

When things go wrong for which you're responsible, your boss's job is to ask you for an explanation.

What your boss doesn't need is for you to blame others, make excuses, or hide the truth.

And yes, the mistake may have been made by one of your team members - not you. But your boss doesn't care. He just wants it fixed.

Here's what your boss expects you to do:

Step 1. Step up and accept the blame!

Step 2. Investigate - what happened and what caused it to happen?

Step 3. Report the facts and recommend how it should be fixed.

Step 4. Fix it and fix it for good!

Step 5. When fixed, report the fix to your boss.

Step 6. Make sure it never happens again.

Accountability is something every boss expects from you but won't tell you until it's too late. Unfortunately, this quality isn't something you were born with. And the only time you get to demonstrate your accountability is when things go wrong.

This also includes the actions, in-actions, and adverse consequences of those members within your charge. You're accountable to your boss for everything that happens or fails to happen within your area of responsibility.

However, *accountability* can't exist unless you know all the things for which you're responsible. For example, you can't be held *accountable* for your company's finances if your duties and responsibilities are to service rental cars.

Establish the reputation of being a good problem solver as well as a good problem finder. Your job is to help your boss find and eliminate all the obstacles that could slow or stop the achievement of his goals.

Remember, mistakes, errors, and defects are not a problem if they're caught and fixed before getting in front of your boss or the customer.

Self-Test
Are you Accountable?

Here are the most important questions to answer to assess your *accountability*.

1. Do you do the right thing?

At an early age, I learned these simple lessons about accountability:

- If you lose, damage, or break something that doesn't belong to you, you need to fix it or buy it.
- If you borrow something, you need to return it in the same or better condition than you found it.
- If you back into and damage someone's car, and they're not around, you need to leave a note on their windshield with your name and phone number to help repair the damage.
- If you were mean or disrespectful to someone, you need to apologize.

2. Are you self-correcting?

A self-correcting person is someone capable of correcting himself without external help.

Part of being *accountable* is being *self-correcting*, especially when starting a new position, even if it's within the same company. Starting anything new is all about learning what you need to know as soon as possible. I'm always amazed by those who never take notes. Why do so few people take notes anymore (with your cell phone or Rocket Book)?

"A short pencil is a long memory." – Unknown.

When you have a question, write it down. Many times, the person with the correct answer won't be immediately available. If you find a term you don't understand, write it down. Later, find out what the term means. Keep a list of all your questions and terms you don't understand.

This list will help later when you sponsor a new member into your team. *Self-correcting* people take notes (they don't trust their memory), write down their questions and the answers, and are not afraid to ask questions and proactively seek answers.

3. Do you live your life with no excuses?

People make excuses because it has worked for them in the past. It avoids accepting *accountability*. They're testing your limits to see how much they can get away with, and they fear the consequences of their actions or inactions.

What's the difference between a reason and an excuse?

Here's a simple rule:

Reasons are believable, understandable, and forgivable.

Excuses aren't.

Here are the commonly used excuses:

- **Denial:** Refusing to admit or acknowledge that their behavior is a problem. (Example: "I can stop swearing any time I want. My language isn't that bad.")

- **Isolation:** Removing themselves from the team area to maintain their behavior. (Example: "If I had my own office, this wouldn't be a problem.")

- **Rationalization:** Giving reasons to explain their behavior. (Example: "I screamed at him because he doesn't like me.")

- **Blaming (or Transferal):** Transferring *accountability* for their behavior to others. (Example: "I wouldn't be late all the time if my teammates treated me right.")

- **Projection:** Rejecting their feelings by ascribing them to another (Example: "Why is that stupid idiot so hostile?")

- **Minimizing or Trivialize:** Refusing to admit the effect of their behavior. (Example: "I only told one bad joke. It's not a big deal.")

They close their eyes to the destructive consequences of their unacceptable behavior, or they explain their actions in a way that saves them from having to feel. Either way, it's wrong and must be dealt with immediately.

4. Do you do your best work every day?

Here's a great story about doing your best work.

> It's rumored that when Dr. **Henry Kissinger** was Secretary of State in the administrations of **Presidents Nixon and Ford**, he asked for a security assessment to be made of a foreign country.
>
> The first day, when a subordinate delivered the report, Secretary Kissinger asked, "Is this your best work?"
>
> The subordinate thought for a second and walked out of the office. The second day, the subordinate returned with the report, and Kissinger asked the same question. The subordinate again thought for a moment and walked back out of the office.
>
> On the third day, the subordinate returned, and Kissinger asked for the third time, "Is this your best work?" This time the subordinate said, "Yes." Kissinger then responded, "Good, now I'll read it."

I share this story to highlight that there are no shortcuts to success. Your success will always be linked to *"doing your best work."* Do you do your best work every day? Would your boss agree?

5. Are you proactive?

Another thing that contributes to your effectiveness and success at work is your ability to be proactive.

A proactive person identifies and prevents potential problems by causing things to happen rather than reacting to them after they happen.

Proactive people:

- Identify potential pre-problems (Chapter 4) before they become a problem and problems before they become a crisis.

- Anticipate their boss's and customer's needs and expectations (Chapter 7).

- Use Preventive Actions (Chapter 4) to identify and resolve all Pre-Problems.

- Take-charge (Chapter 11) and produce order in the midst of chaos.

- Use collaborative problem solving to build consensus (Chapter 23) and resolve Unresolved Issues (Chapter 21)

- Take Immediate Action (Appendix B) and don't wait to be told what to do.

- Anticipate Unintended Consequences and 2d and 3d Order Effects (Chapter 22)

- Manage risk (Chapters 26-28) and make things happen the right way the first time.

6. Do you make recommendations to your boss to make things better?

Your job is to help your boss achieve his goals. What do you do when you find a problem or an improvement that could make things better? Do you create a *Decision Paper* or a *Business Case* (Appendix E) to make it happen?

I've often written Decision Papers through my boss to his boss because my boss didn't have the funding to make it happen. As shown below, the Decision Paper was addressed "To," my boss's boss, "Thru," my boss.

To: My boss's boss.
Thru: My boss.
From: Me

My boss would then initial and write "Approved" next to the "Thru" line above and send it to his boss for final approval. This process helped my boss move the work forward.

7. Do you Apologize with Remorse?

Why is it so hard to say you're sorry or admit a mistake? The answer is simple; you're letting your fear and pride get in your way of doing the right thing.

When your behavior is unacceptable, have the moral courage to apologize, say you're sorry, what you're sorry for, offer no excuse, and don't do it again.

Why no excuses? Making excuses diminishes your sincerity and makes you sound like you're trying to hide behind your excuse. You're human, and humans make mistakes. Express your sincere remorse, not guilt. Guilt is acknowledging your unacceptable behavior, while remorse is regretting your actions and taking steps to undo the damage.

When your finish, look down, say nothing, and wait for a response. The other person doesn't have to forgive you, but you need to forgive yourself and move forward.

There's no excuse for unacceptable behavior.

Guilt leads to destructive tendencies, while remorse leads to constructive actions. To be remorseful, you must accept the guilt first.

Also, when you make a mistake, have the moral courage to admit it, fix it, and learn from it.

If you cannot answer these questions with a strong YES, you need to reassess your *accountability*. Effective people take this assessment annually and fix what needs to be fixed.

This page is intentionally left blank.

ACKNOWLEDGMENTS

"Many people will walk in and out of your life, but only true friends will leave footprints in your heart."
- Eleanor Roosevelt

I'd like to recognize those with whom I've had the pleasure of serving, whose effectiveness and character I vividly recall, many of whom are not here today to tell their story.

For my military career, I thank Betty McIntee, Edward J. Murphy (my Dad), Dale R. Nelson, Geoffrey "Jeff" Prosch, Craig "Randy" Rutler, Dave Wagner, John Andrews, John "The Bear" Warren, John "Jack" Costello, Dan Labin, and Ron Nicholl for their example of effectiveness.

For my coaching career, I thank Tony Robbins, Bernard Haldane, Jack Bissell, Len Drew, Wayne McCullum, Bob Schrier, John Hurtig, and Bob Gerberg for their mentoring and coaching.

Special thanks to my long-time mentor and friend, Joyce Kuntz, who encouraged me to write this book. After leaving the US Military, Joyce was my first and best boss when I joined her consulting firm in Seattle years ago. Unfortunately, Joyce is gone now, but her legacy lives on in this book.

"I must be able to say with sincerity that to see things differently is a strength, not a weakness, in my relationship with others."
- Joyce Kuntz

I thank Joyce's husband, Ed Kuntz, who turned out to be the man who brought me to Seattle from Kansas City to start my incredible second career as an Executive Coach.

And finally, I thank my soulmate and wife, *Diana*, for her love, encouragement, and understanding throughout this process.

When I count my blessings, I always count her twice.

This page is intentionally left blank.

ABOUT THE AUTHOR

"I expect to pass through this world but once; any good thing therefore that I can do, or any kindness that I can show to any fellow creature, let me do it now; let me not defer or neglect it, for I shall not pass this way again."
- Stephan Grelle

Ed Murphy considers himself lucky. From age 7, he knew what he wanted to be when he grew up. He wanted to be a Soldier. So, four days after graduating from High School, he joined the US Army and found himself in Basic Training and Advanced Infantry Training at Fort Dix, New Jersey.

A year later, Ed became a Cadet at the United States Military Academy at West Point. In 1970, he graduated as a 2d Lieutenant headed to Airborne and Ranger School, then off to Viet Nam for a year.

In 1978, Ed returned to West Point to teach Military Science and earned an MS from LIU in night school. During his tenure as a Battalion Commander in West Germany, his greatest achievement was helping 1400 soldiers begin a college education. He wanted to give his soldiers something of real value - something that no one could ever take away. After 23 years as a US Army Officer, he retired in 1993.

For his second career, with help from *Tony Robbins*, he became an Executive Coach. Then, for the next 21 years, he worked for four of the largest career development and outplacement companies in America, from Seattle, San Diego, Kansas City, and Phoenix.

In 2012, Ed retired a second time and decided to document everything he learned from those he most admired during his 50+ years in the US Military as an Army Officer and Corporate America as an Executive Coach.

In 2014, he began writing books for Amazon and Kindle dedicated to providing the best-in-class wisdom, knowledge, and advice to help others maximize their true career potential by becoming more effective and successful at work and in life.

Today, Ed considers himself blessed to live in Phoenix, AZ. He enjoys writing, eating sushi, genealogy, and watching movies with family, friends, and his best friend and wife, *Diana*.

CONCLUSION

Congratulations!

And thank you for joining us on this *Journey of Discovery*.

As promised, you now have a *Delegating Guide* to add to your professional library - the one I never had.

Every effective boss needs effective followers who can consistently produce excellent results and add value to those who helped produce those results.

You now have the most actionable *Delegating Skills* you were never taught in school or college to support you throughout your career.

Now it's your turn to apply and share this new knowledge to add greater value to your boss and all those with whom you serve.

These are the essential *Best Practices* I've learned over the past 50 years to help you become far more effective and successful than you were yesterday.

As always, I wish you great success.

Never STOP Learning!

Ed

Founder of *The Effectiveness Institute*

email: ed.murphy77@gmail.com

PS: Also, if you feel this information could help someone else, please let them know. If it turns out to make a difference in their life, they'll be forever grateful to you, as will I.

Stop wishing you were better and do something about it today.

www.ingramcontent.com/pod-product-compliance
Lightning Source LLC
Chambersburg PA
CBHW051914170526
45168CB00001B/384